THE
LITTLE
BOOK
OF
BRUNCH

Caroline Craig & Sophie Missing

THE LITTLE BOOK OF BRUNCH

Easy & inspiring recipes for the day's best meal

Introduction - 6

1 - The Classics - 8

2 - Modern Medleys - 46

3 - Tartines, Toasties and Sandwiches - 68

4 - Quick Ideas for One or Two - 88

5 - Bottomless Brunch - 100

6 - Fresh and Light(er) - 126

7 - Savouries - 142

8 - That Sweet Spot - 156

9 - Extras - 174

10 - Hair of the Dog and Thirst Quenchers - 196

Index - 212

Acknowledgements - 220

About the Authors - 222

Introduction

The Little Book of Brunch is a collection of recipes for what many consider to be the best meal of the day.

But what's the deal with brunch – why is the breakfast-lunch composite so increasingly popular?

Brunch isn't about shoehorning another meal into the day. As two people who write about food and love cooking, we're pretty keen eaters, but even we draw the line at having breakfast, brunch, lunch and dinner (at least, not on a regular basis – major holidays excepted). But brunch we do, and often too. For us, it almost always takes the place of both breakfast and lunch, and while of course it's lovely to go out for the occasion sometimes, given the simplicity of many of the dishes on offer (avocado, coffee, eggs, toast) we often end up wondering what feasts we could have conjured up at home for the same price – and without having to scramble to secure a table.

Brunch is about simple, unpretentious yet delicious fare. It's a meal that allows you to gorge on bread without being judged (who's to know you're not doing a 10K later?), to be able to cook food for those you love without spending or slaving too much, or simply to treat yourself to a good, nourishing, homemade meal, even if you missed breakfast.

Unlike, say, Sunday lunch, a weekend brunch holds all the promise of the day(s) ahead. It can provide the stomach-lining foundation for afternoons and nights out, or the carb-laced stupor for hours spent lolling on the sofa.

The timing of the meal itself is perfect. If it's the morning after a 'Late One' (we use the word 'morning' loosely here), anyone you are cooking for will be grateful that they are not expected either to wake up or come over first thing. Brunch always perfectly coincides with raging hunger pangs: after all, hangovers wait for no lunch.

But what to cook for your perfectly orchestrated and satiating banquet?

Brunch can incorporate classic breakfast ingredients (eggs, sausages, toast), or be a riff on something you might think firmly lunch or dinner territory (an Indian breakfast curry, pizza or a fluffy jacket potato, say).

It can be as fancy or frugal as you like: you can splash out on sushi-grade salmon and invest the time in curing it yourself – this costs about £6, so is not prohibitively expensive, but still a treat and it sounds lavish, doesn't it? Or you can spend £2 on tinned beans and jazz them up with spices to make a ful medames in 20 minutes.

It can be boozy or abstemious: you can crack out the cocktails and let brunch segue seamlessly into dinner, or you can have an enjoyable break from everything before continuing your day.

It's almost endlessly adaptable: there are as many different ingredients you can add to your scrambled eggs as there are schools of thought on how best to cook them. Don't have any coriander? Use something else – or leave it out. Have a carrot you want to use up? Go ahead and grate it into your potato pancakes. Brunch is the meal when you can get away with anything.

It's also accessible; with the exception of a very few recipes involving curing, slow overnight cooking or proving, which do require some pre-planning, most of the recipes in this book can be made spontaneously – our favourite way to cook.

Brunch can be a delightfully enjoyable way of catching up with those you love. Cooking brunch for friends and family is entertaining without the stress, expense or copious amounts of wine that a three-course dinner can involve. At brunch, people are generally happiest with coffee, juice, eggs and frequently replenished stacks of buttered toast. But equally, if you wish, you can spend a little extra on treat items. With a chunk of 'nduja sausage, some salmon or a posh sourdough loaf, often a little goes a long way. It all depends on the sort of affair you're planning.

There's the hours-long Saturday morning brunch we have every couple of months with a group of friends, where we take turns to have people over. At these leisurely meals we might eat rhubarb compote, yoghurt and a little granola in small glasses to start, followed by boiled eggs, toast and a bit of cured ham if we're feeling flush. This brunch might end in a gentle stroll through a local park – though it might just as easily descend into drunken chaos and impromptu karaoke.

A weekday brunch is a wholly different affair, by necessity speedier and involving fewer components. It might be tinned chickpeas sautéed with some green veg and topped with a fried egg, or some avocado squidged onto sourdough toast, seasoned with lemon juice, sea salt and chilli flakes (forgive us this cliché; it does taste good). Whatever we eat, this type of brunch is a much-needed moment of peaceful enjoyment savoured between

whatever else is going on during the day. This versatility is what can make brunch the most appealing of meals; it's a moveable feast.

You can, of course, also cook the recipes in this book at any time of day, which brings us back to the fundamental joy of brunch: there really are no rules. Whether you're cooking for yourself, your housemates, family, partner or friends, when in doubt keep it simple – or wing it.

The history of brunch

Many people think of brunch as a modern invention – the more cynical might see it as an excuse for restaurants to charge a tenner for two tepid poached eggs. But the word was first used in an 1895 article in the (unsurprisingly now defunct) British magazine *Hunter's Weekly*: 'Brunch,' journalist Guy Beringer wrote, 'is cheerful, sociable and inciting. It puts you in a good temper… it sweeps away the worries and cobwebs of the week.'

These days we are more likely to use our toast to scoop up shakshuka than the potted pigeon from hunters' brunch banquets of yore, but the spirit of the thing remains the same. A good brunch does put you in a happy mood; it can be the most sociable of meals. But there is also something in the very act of carving out the time for it that does sweep away mortal worries – if only for a brief period.

Dishes from early twentieth-century British 'savoury' courses were traditionally served at the end of a meal as a precursor to the cheese course, and often celebrated what are now staple brunch items: kippers with bread and butter, Welsh rabbit etc. We've included a chapter of these recipes as they are definitely due for a revival.

Brunches of the world

More than any other meal, perhaps, brunch is a multicultural mash-up. We are extremely lucky to have access to more specialist ingredients from around the world than ever before and, what's more, the knowledge of what to do with them. Gone are the days when olive oil could only be bought over the chemist's counter. But we're also becoming more open to the delicious, usually savoury, breakfast dishes enjoyed in many countries outside the Western world. It might feel a stretch to eat a spicy potato curry for breakfast (personally, we're very into it) but serve it at brunch and no one will bat an eyelid.

Condiments are key

There are times in posh restaurants when you're made to feel like a savage for requesting some ketchup. Of all the meals, brunch is probably the occasion when condiments and seasoning are not only welcome but absolutely necessary. A crucial part of the joy of the thing is customising whatever you're eating, whether it's a liberal shake of hot sauce on your eggs or a sprinkle of capers on your bagel. There's nothing so disappointing as being made a bacon sandwich and then having to politely endure the devastating news that your hosts don't have your beloved brown sauce. Don't be that person: hoard sauces, relishes and jams, even if you don't use them that often. They keep for ages – you're probably given a few every Christmas, and if you are light-fingered, you can procure mini jars from hotel buffet breakfasts. Laying out an array of condiments on your table – or on a tray in proper B&B style – takes 30 seconds but makes it look like you've put on a real spread.

Here are our favourite squeezes, sprinkles and spreads:

- Sea salt and a fully loaded pepper grinder (this is also the time to crack out any novelty items you might have lurking in your fridge like, say, smoked salt – brunch is a great way to clear out your cupboards)
- Dried chilli flakes
- Chilli sauce (Encona, Sriracha, Cholula, Frank's, El Yucateco Green Habanero, Tabasco… we have literally about 20 different hot sauces on the go at any one time)
- Honey (if you can, try to get one that is local and not made from a blend of honeys)
- Marmite (or, you know, Vegemite)
- Peanut butter
- Tomato ketchup
- HP sauce
- Colman's English mustard
- Dijon and/or wholegrain mustard
- Assorted pickles and chutneys
- Jam (apricot, raspberry)
- Marmalade
- Cream cheese (obligatory for bagels)
- Mayonnaise (see page 194 for how to make your own)

Cook's notes

Unless otherwise stated

- All eggs are medium.
- All black pepper is freshly ground.
- We use Maldon sea salt.

Perfect Eggs

Brunch doesn't have to contain eggs, but it often does.

At least with eggs, unlike meat, there's a ceiling of around £3 for free range and organic. Eggs bought from a farm shop are the bucolic dream, but we also like to treat ourselves to Clarence Court eggs (available from major supermarkets), which have a vibrant orange yolk.

Unless otherwise indicated in a recipe, we use medium eggs and keep them at room temperature – storing them in the fridge will affect the cooking times given in the recipes. Obviously, use whatever size eggs you have, but bear in mind that the cooking times should be slightly longer when, say, boiling a large egg.

Ideally, you want to use eggs that are as fresh as possible. This is particularly important when poaching, as the whites of older eggs don't hold together so well. Unfortunately, it's difficult to have much control over this when shopping – as the great M.F.K. Fisher noted, 'the finest way to know your egg is fresh is to own the hen that makes it'. For all of us non-hen owners then, if you want to test how fresh your eggs are, put them in a tall glass of water: a fresh egg will remain at the bottom, but a less fresh one will float. So: how do you like your eggs in the morning?

Fried

We love a crispy-edged (sorry, Elizabeth David) fried egg, with a runny yolk that has none of that unpalatable uncooked white still clinging to its top.

Add oil with a fairly high smoking point (e.g. sunflower, vegetable or olive oil) to a frying pan and put over a medium to high heat. When hot – not smoking or spitting, but hot enough that you can feel the heat rising if you hold your palm above the pan – carefully crack in your egg(s). Fry for around 2–3 minutes. If you have a lid for your pan, you could put this on after a minute, as the steam will help to cook the egg surface slightly – sort of like an 'over easy' egg, but without the faff of actually flipping it.

Scrambled

Whisk the eggs (usually 2 per person) with a pinch of salt and a twist of pepper. Add a knob of butter to a pan and put over a medium to low heat. Once melted, turn the heat down ever so slightly and add the egg mix. Using a wooden spoon, stir fairly continuously, scraping the bottom of the pan, until you achieve a good scrambled egg consistency: cooked through, but still creamy.

Boiled

There are many schools of thought on how to boil an egg. If you have a trusted method, great; if it ain't broke, don't fix it. Many may disagree but we always cook our eggs in water that is already boiling – it works for us. If you aren't going to eat your boiled egg immediately (and, if not, why not? There are few things in life that are more delicious than a just-boiled egg), drain it and leave in cool water to stop it from continuing to cook. See over page for our tried-and-tested timings: these are for room-temperature eggs that have been added to a pan of boiling water.

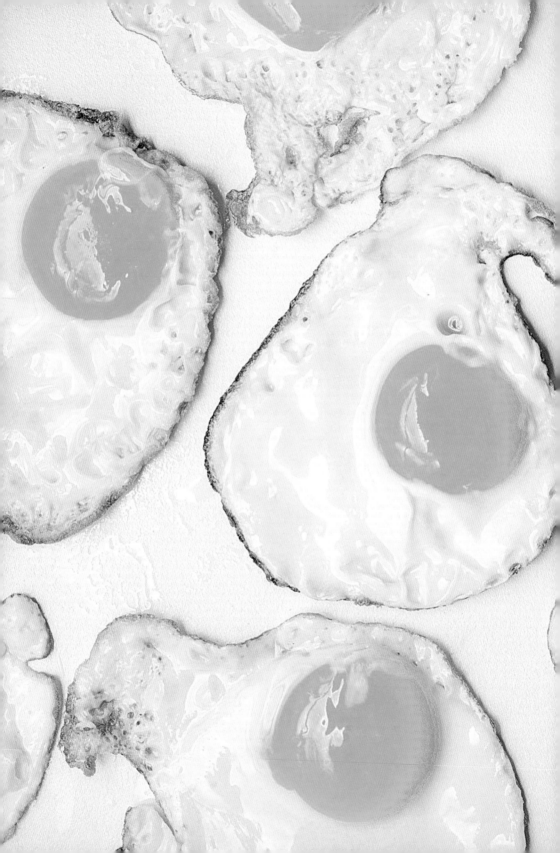

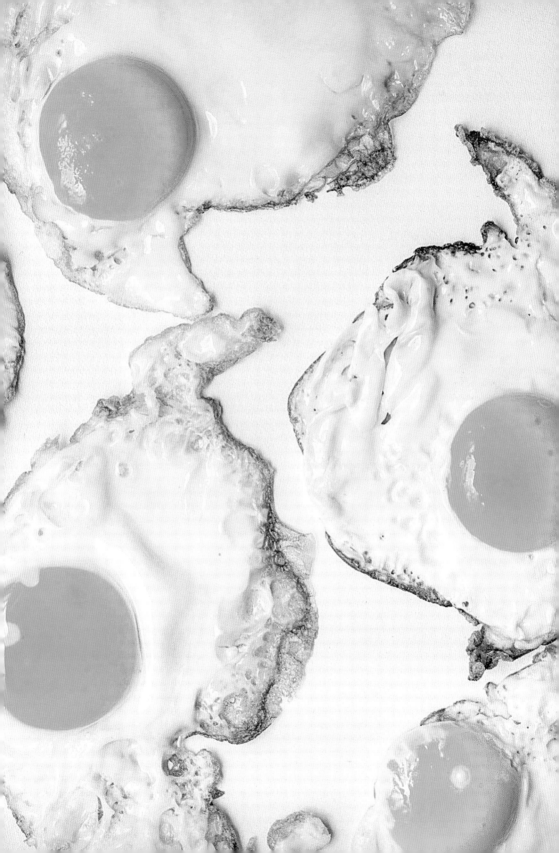

Soft (dippy):
Cook for exactly 6 minutes
Medium (ever so slightly runny):
Cook for exactly 7 minutes
'Fudgy yolked' (a personal favourite):
Cook for exactly 8 minutes
Hard (not runny at all):
Cook for exactly 9 minutes

Poached

Poaching can feel like a fool's errand,
something better left to the experts. But it
is possible to make a poached egg at home,
though it may not look quite as perfect as
one you eat at, say, the Wolseley. Here's
how to crack on.

Add water to a small pan so that it is about
a third full. Put over a medium heat until
it starts to simmer (i.e. when you can see
bubbles). You can add a tablespoon
of vinegar at this point, if you like.

Crack an egg into a small glass, then
carefully pour into the water. With a small
spoon, gently swirl the water around the
egg to create a whirlpool effect – this will
encourage the white to hold together and
not stick to the bottom of the pan.

Cook for 1½ minutes, then remove with a
slotted spoon and drain on kitchen paper
before seasoning and serving.

Coddled

Somewhere in between boiling and
poaching, coddling involves cooking an
egg very gently in a bain marie of simmering
water. It's the kind of thing you might imagine
being fed to an Edwardian invalid swaddled
in blankets and lying on a chaise-longue.

To lovingly coddle an egg, you'll need a
coddler, a wonderfully retro bit of kitchen
kit (essentially, small lidded pots made of
porcelain or glass).

Crack a room-temperature egg into your
coddler and then submerge it in a pan of
simmering water – you want the water to
just cover the coddler with the handle sitting
above it. Cook for around 7 minutes, or until
you have a softly set white and still runny
yolk. Carefully remove the coddler from the
water by its handle.

You can add spices or even a little cream to
your coddler if you want to jazz up your egg.
Serve with the ultimate nursery food: hot
buttered soldiers.

1

The Classics

Eggs Benedict

The ultimate brunch choice: some hollandaise, a muffin, ham and two eggs. Perfection. We've included our own recipe for English muffins on page 185 and, we promise, most of the work is done the night before, so they are almost ready to bake come morning… but… but… if you don't want to go the whole hog, just give yourself a break and buy them. The one thing you shouldn't worm your way out of, however, is making your own hollandaise. Just do it.

Preparation time: 35 minutes
Cooking time: 25 minutes
Serves: 4

1 quantity of hollandaise (see page 195)
4 English muffins (shop-bought
   or homemade, see page 185)

4 slices of cooked ham, cut in half
splash of white wine vinegar
8 eggs
1 tsp smoked paprika

Preheat the oven to 140°C/gas 1.

Meanwhile, make the hollandaise, which should take about 15 minutes. Keep warm.

Halve and toast the muffins, then place in the warmed oven, piled on top of four plates, along with the ham (placed in a small separate dish, covered with foil).

Now attend to your poached eggs. Pop two large pans, filled with 8cm water, on to boil, and once bubbling, lower to a simmer and add a splash of white wine vinegar to each pan. Then, as quickly and carefully as you can, crack 4 eggs into one pan, then 4 eggs into the other. Put a timer on for 2 minutes.

While the eggs are poaching, cover a large plate with kitchen paper, ready for blotting them. Remove the warmed plates from the oven and place two muffin halves on each one. Butter them, then cover each half with an artfully rolled piece of warmed ham.

Once the timer is up, quickly remove the eggs from the first pan using a slotted spoon and place on the paper-lined plate. Repeat with the eggs from the second pan. Once you are satisfied you have removed much of the water, pop a poached egg on each muffin half. Top with generous dollops of hollandaise and a sprinkling of paprika. Scoff immediately.

Shakshuka

This hugely popular Middle Eastern breakfast dish is good enough to eat at any time of day, sitting comfortably in the Breakfast for Dinner camp. The easiest way to ensure you have perfect runny yolks is to use a sauté or frying pan for which you have a lid (ideally glass) so that they steam slightly.

Preparation time: 5–10 minutes
Cooking time: 30 minutes
Serves: 2

1 tbsp neutral oil, such as rapeseed
1 onion, halved then sliced into
    thin half-moons
large pinch of sea salt
large pinch of sugar
2 peppers, seeded and sliced
    into thin strips
1 tsp cumin seeds, roughly crushed
    using a pestle and mortar

¼ tsp smoked paprika
large pinch of pul biber
    (or regular chilli flakes)
½ cinnamon stick
1 x 400g tin plum tomatoes
4–6 eggs (depending how hungry you are)

To serve
crumbled labneh
pul biber (or regular chilli flakes)
bread (sourdough, flatbread, challah,
    tortilla wraps – whatever you like)

Put a frying or sauté pan over a medium heat and add the oil. Once hot, add the onion, salt and sugar and fry, stirring occasionally, for 5 minutes or until coloured and softening. Add the peppers and stir, then continue to fry for 10 minutes until they are cooked through but still holding their shape; add a splash of water halfway through to stop them from burning. Stir in the spices and fry for a couple of minutes. Pour in the tomatoes, crushing them in your hand before they hit the pan, and removing any hard stalky bits. Half-fill the empty tin with water and pour into the pan to use up all the tomato juice.

Lower the heat slightly and cook, uncovered, for 10–12 minutes until reduced. Taste and adjust the seasoning as necessary, or add a little more water if it has reduced too much.

Reduce the heat to medium to low then make four to six wells in the pan. Swiftly crack an egg into each well and put the lid on the pan. Cook for 4½–5 minutes – until the egg whites are just set and the yolks are still runny. You can test this by gently pressing down on them with your finger: there should be no goo on the whites and the yolks should feel springy and wobbly.

Sprinkle labneh and extra chilli flakes on top and serve immediately, with bread for mopping up the yolks and sauce.

Masala Omelette

Delicious with plenty of buttered toast
and some extra hot sauce, or with a dollop
of labneh (see page 193) or Greek yoghurt.

Preparation time: 6 minutes
Cooking time: 5 minutes
Serves: 1

2 eggs
splash of milk
¼ tsp ground turmeric

½ tsp curry powder
½ tbsp olive oil
¼ red onion
½ red chilli
4 sprigs of fresh coriander
½ tomato
pinch of salt and black pepper

Crack the eggs into a bowl. Add the milk
followed by the spices and a pinch of salt
and pepper. Whisk to combine. Set aside.

Place the olive oil in a small frying pan over
a medium heat. Chop the onion, chilli,
coriander and tomato as finely as you can.
Add the vegetables to the pan and cook for
a minute or so to soften.

Turn the heat up slightly and, using a
wooden spatula, spread the ingredients
about so they are evenly distributed.

Pour the egg mixture in, tilting the pan
for equal coverage, and, after about 30
seconds, use the spatula again to coax
the edges down a little.

After another 30 seconds, use the spatula
to have a peek at the underside of the
omelette. If it looks nice and golden, fold
about a third of the omelette towards the
middle on both sides so you have something
resembling a rectangle, albeit with curved
short ends. Cook for a further 20 seconds,
then slide onto a plate. Enjoy immediately.

Overnight Boston Baked Beans

The idea is to make these the night before your brunch, just before you go to bed… they will bubble away in the oven over a low heat and, come morning, you will have something gorgeous, substantial and seemingly complex to serve your guests.

The only advance prep you'll need to do is soak the beans: using dried beans is key here as they hold their texture, even after being cooked for 8 hours. Don't be tempted to add any salt until just before you eat as this can cause the skins to toughen.

Preparation time: 5 minutes, plus 8 hours soaking
Cooking time: 8 hours
Serves: 8

500g dried cannellini beans
800g pork belly
2 x 400g tins plum tomatoes
2 garlic cloves

1 heaped tbsp black treacle
1 tsp cloves
3 bay leaves
3 tbsp mustard
2 tsp smoked paprika
750ml stock
salt and black pepper
8 slices of buttered, toasted sourdough, to serve

Place the beans in a large bowl and cover with plenty of water. Leave to soak for about half a day (or longer).

The night before your brunch, when you are about to go to bed, preheat the oven to 140°C/gas ½. Take a large, lidded casserole dish (preferably cast-iron) and add the soaked and drained beans.

Chop the pork belly into chunks and add to the casserole, followed by the tinned tomatoes, crushing them with your fingers as you pour them in. Add the whole garlic cloves, followed by the treacle, cloves, bay leaves, mustard, paprika and stock. Season with pepper, mix well, then pop the lid on and place in the oven. Cook for 8 hours.

In the morning, take the casserole from the oven and remove the lid. Oven temperatures do vary, so if there is too much liquid in the pan, place on the hob (lid off) over a medium heat and continue to cook until you have a lovely thick consistency. Keep warm or reheat just before you are ready to eat.

Season to taste before serving on buttered sourdough.

Cheese, Ham and Egg Buckwheat Galettes

The holy trinity of fillings that is cheese, ham and egg is known as a *galette complète* in Brittany, where these savoury pancakes come from.

Resting the batter for an hour in the fridge does make for a lighter pancake – or you can make it in advance and leave overnight. The galettes themselves can be made a couple of hours ahead, if necessary. Keep them warm, then add the filling and bake just before eating. A mustardy little gem salad is the perfect accompaniment.

Preparation time: 5 minutes, plus chilling
Cooking time: 30 minutes
Serves: 4

200g buckwheat flour
¼ tsp fine sea salt

525ml milk
2 eggs
butter, for frying
200g Comté or Gruyère cheese, grated
16 slices of ham
8 eggs
salt and black pepper

In a bowl, whisk together the flour and salt then gradually add in the milk. Whisk in the eggs one by one until all incorporated. Cover with cling film and leave for 1 hour in the fridge.

If you have a pancake pan, use that – if not, a flat cast-iron or non-stick frying pan will do fine. Place over a medium heat, add a little butter to melt (not too much) and cover the base. When you can feel the heat coming off the pan, lower the heat ever so slightly and spoon in 3–4 tablespoons of batter then swirl the pan quickly so that the batter forms a nice round pancake shape. Cook for 1½ minutes, then flip and cook for another 1–1½ minutes. Transfer to a plate and cover with greaseproof paper. Repeat until you've used up all the batter and have a stack of 8 pancakes.

When you're almost ready to eat, preheat the oven to 200°C/gas 6. Lightly grease a couple of baking trays and line with baking paper.

Place a pancake on one of the prepared trays and top with a couple of slices of ham. Add about 25g of the cheese, then use your finger to push it out from the middle and build up a circular 'rampart' (this will stop the egg leaking onto the pancake). Carefully crack an egg into the middle of the cheese crater. Fold each side of the pancake in on itself so you can just see a square of the filling and egg in the centre. Repeat this step with the remaining pancakes.

Cook in the oven for 12–15 minutes until the whites of the eggs are set. Season and serve with some mustardy salad leaves.

Baked Arnie Bennie Eggs

A delicious baked take on the omlette Arnold Bennett. The hollandaise makes this more of a weekend affair, so put on BBC Radio 4's Saturday Live and whisk exuberantly.

Preparation time: 10 minutes
Cooking time: 15 minutes
Serves: 4

250ml hollandaise (ideally homemade, see page 195)
butter, for greasing

8 eggs
120g smoked haddock
black pepper
buttered toast, to serve

Preheat the oven to 140°C/gas 1.

Meanwhile, make the hollandaise then set aside and keep warm.

Grease four 16cm pie dishes with the butter. Crack 2 eggs in each. Chop the haddock into small chunks and distribute between the dishes. Add a few twists of black pepper, cover with foil and bake in the oven for 12 minutes.

After 12 minutes have passed, remove the dishes from the oven and discard the foil. Spoon over the hollandaise and return to the oven for a further 3–4 minutes.

Enjoy immediately with buttered toast.

Baked Eggs with Asparagus

Like the Baked Arnie Bernie Eggs, this dish is luxurious, more befitting a linen napkin setting than kitchen paper.

Preparation time: 10 minutes
Cooking time: 20 minutes
Serves: 4

250ml hollandaise (ideally homemade, see page 195)

100g asparagus tips
butter, for greasing
8 eggs
salt and black pepper
buttered toast, to serve

Preheat the oven to 140°C/gas 1.

Meanwhile, make the hollandaise then set aside and keep warm.

Place a pan of salted water on to boil and, once bubbling, blanch the asparagus for a few minutes. Grease four 16cm pie dishes with the butter. Crack 2 eggs in each. Distribute the asparagus tips between the dishes – usually about three per person. Add a few twists of black pepper, cover with foil and bake in the oven for 12 minutes.

After 12 minutes have passed, remove the dishes from the oven and discard the foil. Spoon over the hollandaise and return to the oven for a further 3–4 minutes.

Enjoy immediately with buttered toast.

Baked Bennie

We end this trio of baked egg recipes with the simplest. Any ham will do to be honest, but there is nothing like the decent cured variety in our opinion.

Preparation time: 10 minutes
Cooking time: 15 minutes
Serves: 4

250ml hollandaise (ideally homemade, see page 195)

butter, for greasing
8 eggs
100g cured ham, such as Bayonne or Serrano
black pepper
buttered toast, to serve

Preheat the oven to 140°C/gas 1.

Meanwhile, make the hollandaise then set aside and keep warm.

Grease four 16cm pie dishes with the butter. Crack 2 eggs into each. Rip the ham a little and distribute between the dishes. Add a few twists of black pepper, cover with foil and bake in the oven for 12 minutes. After 12 minutes have passed, remove the dishes from the oven and discard the foil. Spoon over the hollandaise and return to the oven for a further 3–4 minutes.

Enjoy immediately with buttered toast.

Brioche French Toast

You can of course use any bread you like here, but a thick wodge of brioche feels especially indulgent. We love to eat this with a generous spoonful of sour cherry compote (see page 167).

Preparation time: 2 minutes
Cooking time: 5 minutes
Serves: 1 (just multiply the ingredients to serve more)

1 egg
little splash of milk
1 tbsp unwaxed lemon zest

sprinkle of vanilla caster sugar
butter, for frying
1 thick slice (3cm-ish) of brioche or other bread

To serve
Icing sugar and sour cherry compote (see page 167) or fresh fruit and berries

---

Crack the egg into a wide flattish bowl and whisk. Add the milk, lemon zest and sugar and whisk thoroughly to combine.

Put a frying pan over a medium heat and add the butter. While it melts, dip the bread into the eggy mix. When the bread is well soaked and the butter in the pan is hot, add the bread, pouring over any excess egg mixture. Fry for a couple of minutes on each side until golden and crisp.

Serve immediately, with a dusting of icing sugar and compote or some fresh fruit.

Pancake or Waffle Buttermilk Batter

This batter recipe makes pancakes or waffles that are crisp on the outside and fluffy on the inside. Keep it simple and serve them dotted with butter and drizzled with maple syrup, with some fresh fruit on the side, or use the basic batter ('basic' here is a boon) as a building block to which you can add extra elements like berries or chocolate chips... We've listed a few of our favourite flavour combinations below, although freestyling with the contents of your fridge is part of the fun.

You can cook your pancakes or waffles in advance and place them on a greaseproof paper-lined baking tray, ready to warm through in the oven before serving. But (as is often the case with fried things) they are best eaten straight from the pan. Try not to burn your mouth, though.

Preparation time: 5 minutes
Cooking time: 5–6 minutes per
  pancake or waffle
Serves: 4 (2 waffles or pancakes each)

125g plain flour
1 tbsp caster sugar
½ tsp salt
1 tsp baking powder
½ tsp bicarbonate of soda
280ml buttermilk
1 egg
30g butter, melted and cooled

vegetable oil, for frying/greasing
butter and maple syrup, to serve

Optional extras

- 2 bananas, roughly mashed, plus the seeds of ½ vanilla pod
- 150g fresh or frozen raspberries, blueberries or other summer fruit, plus the zest of ½ lemon
- 100g ricotta, plus the zest of ½ orange
- 120g grated cheese, plus a pinch of cayenne pepper (omit the sugar)

Whisk all the dry ingredients together in a large bowl. Make a well in the centre and gradually mix the buttermilk, eggs and butter together until incorporated – it's okay if the butter is a bit lumpy. Stir in any optional extras at this point. Cover and refrigerate for 30 minutes or until chilled.

For pancakes
Heat a well-greased cast-iron or non-stick pan over a medium to low heat. When hot, add a tablespoon of oil and swirl it around. Add a tablespoon of batter and spread out with a palette knife or knife to a circle about 10–12cm in diameter. Cook for around 3 minutes on each side (the time will depend on the size of your pancakes), using a metal spatula to flip over when browned. If they're colouring too quickly turn the heat down a little.

For waffles
Lightly grease and heat a waffle iron/maker. Add a tablespoon of batter to each waffle mould, smoothing over so that they are evenly filled – don't overfill. Cook for about 5 minutes until brown and very crisp.

Scottish-style Porridge

Everyone is different but for us, 50g of
porridge per person is more than enough.
The quantities below make enough for four
lovely little bowls of the good stuff.

Preparation time: 1 minute
Cooking time: 20 minutes
Serves: 4

200g jumbo porridge oats
generous pinch of salt
600ml water, plus extra if needed
warmed milk, to serve

Add the oats, salt and water to a pan and
place over a low heat. Bring to a very gentle
simmer, stirring frequently with a wooden
spoon, and adding splashes of extra water
as you go if need be: you're aiming for a
lovely thick and creamy consistency. Divide
between four bowls and cover with warmed
milk. Garnish as desired.

Optional extras

- chopped apple, brown sugar and
  a pinch of cinnamon and nutmeg
- nutella and chopped toasted hazelnuts
- lavender honey and flaked almonds
- chopped peach and poppy seeds

A Veggie Fry-Up with Homemade Hash Brown

For us, a rösti-inspired hash brown is the main event in any veggie fry-up. Here it is pre-fried, then warmed in the oven until you're about to serve, taking the pressure off somewhat. As with any fry-up, timing is key: start with the hash brown, then attend to the rest.

Preparation time: 15 minutes
Cooking time: 30 minutes
Serves: 4

800g waxy potatoes, unpeeled
4 tbsp sunflower oil
large knob of butter

2 tbsp olive oil
4 tomatoes, halved horizontally
4 eggs
2 avocados
1 lemon, halved
salt and pepper

Preheat the oven to 160°C/gas 3.

Coarsely grate the potatoes, then squeeze out as much moisture as you can with your hands (over kitchen paper or the sink). Transfer to a colander, sprinkle over some salt and pepper and set aside for a couple of minutes.

Place half the oil in a non-stick ovenproof frying pan and place over a medium heat. Once the oil is hot (test it by throwing in a little bit of potato, which should sizzle, but not too wildly), take a handful of potato, give it a further squeeze, then loosely sprinkle into the pan. Working quickly, continue squeezing and sprinkling potato until you have used it all up. Use a spatula to pat around the 'cake' to make it circular, then slide it underneath to loosen the bottom and ensure it is not sticking. Leave for a few minutes to seal, then turn the heat down and repeat every now and then until the underside has turned golden and smells cooked (about 7 minutes).

Remove the pan from the heat. Place a large plate on top and flip the pan over so the hash brown sits on it cooked-side-up.

Place the pan back over a medium heat and add the remaining oil. Once hot, carefully slide the cake back into the pan to cook the underside. Again, leave to seal for a few minutes, then turn the heat down and use the spatula to pat around the 'cake' and loosen it from the bottom of the pan. Continue cooking until golden on the underside and cooked through (about 7–10 minutes).

About 5–10 minutes before serving, pop the hash brown into the oven to keep warm while you attend to your tomatoes and eggs.

Place one frying pan on the hob over a medium heat and add a tablespoon of the olive oil. Place the halved tomatoes in the pan, sprinkle over some salt and pepper and fry for 5 minutes on each side. Five minutes in, place another pan on the hob over a

(continued overleaf)

medium heat and add the remaining olive oil.

Crack in the eggs and cook to your liking (sunny side up is always pleasing to the eye).

Stone, peel and slice the avocados, then divide between four plates. Squeeze over some fresh lemon juice and a sprinkling of salt.

Remove the hash brown from the oven. Using a spatula, slide it out onto a chopping board, for ease, then cut into slices. Divide between the plates, placing a fried egg and 2 tomato halves alongside.

Classy Chip Butty

Somehow the use of pittas and sweet potatoes make a chip butty more acceptable in polite company.

Preparation time: 10 minutes
Cooking time: 40 minutes
Serves: 4

3 large sweet potatoes
5 garlic cloves
4 bay leaves
3 tbsp extra-virgin olive oil
4 pitta breads
2 tbsp chopped fresh parsley
salt and black pepper

For the garlic butter
20g butter
2 garlic cloves, crushed

For the tahini
4 tbsp tahini
juice of 1 lemon

Preheat the oven to 200°C/gas 6.

Cut the sweet potatoes into even-sized wedges, keeping the skin on, and place in a baking tray. Bash the garlic, again keeping the skin on, and distribute, along with the bay leaves, in the tray. Drizzle over the olive oil, then add some salt and pepper. Roast in the oven for about 30 minutes, or until the potatoes are lovely and crispy in parts, with soft centres.

While the potatoes are cooking, place the butter and crushed garlic in a small pan and melt over a low heat. Mix, then set aside until you are ready to serve.

Spoon the tahini into a bowl, add the lemon juice and a few tablespoons of tepid water, mixing as you go, until you have a fairly wet but creamy consistency. Taste to check the seasoning.

When the potatoes are ready, set them aside. Pop the pittas in the oven and bake for a few minutes until just warmed through (you want to be able to open and stuff them without any cracking). Now halve them and, taking one side at a time, open the pockets and spread the insides liberally with the garlic butter, followed by dollops of tahini. Next, stuff them with the potato wedges and finish with a final drizzle of tahini and a sprinkling of chopped parsley.

Enjoy!

Heat the oven on to 180°C/gas 4. Next put the kettle on and make yourself a cup of tea. Now unpack the sausages and place in a large ovenproof dish. Pop in the oven and cook for 35 minutes, turning occasionally. During the first 10 minutes of cooking time, lay the table with condiments and plates.

F
R
I
L
L
S

With 25 minutes still to go, place your largest frying pan (or two smaller ones) over a medium heat and drizzle in plenty of olive oil. Add the tomatoes, sprinkle with salt and pepper and cook for about 5 minutes on both sides. Push them to the side of the pan and add the bacon (plus more oil if needed).

F
U
L
L

Fry for a few minutes on both sides until just turning crispy, then chuck in the oven along with the tomatoes, into the dish with your sizzling sausages.

E
N
G
L
I
S
H

Heat the beans in a pan and pop over a medium heat and put someone in charge of toasting bread. Add more oil to the initial frying pan and crack in the eggs. Cook for a few minutes, then serve alongside the oven goods. Probably best to offer the beans separately rather than dish out because – as our friend Felicity Cloake would say there are firm non-bean-Beliebers out there.

② Modern Medleys

Potato Bhaji with Cecina

Potato curry for breakfast – surely this has to be one of the best things about being in India. Traditionally served with wholemeal deep-fried puffed breads, here we've opted for chickpea chapatis (aka cecina) as they are easier to make, probably healthier and, of course, delicious.

We wouldn't serve up huge amounts of curry here – this isn't a Friday night takeaway – just a little bowl with a pancake for dunking and scooping up the delicious stew. Serve with soft-boiled eggs and some fresh fruit on the side (perhaps one of the fruit salads on page 140).

Preparation time: 10 minutes
Cooking time: 30 minutes
Serves: 4

For the curry
1kg floury potatoes, larger ones halved
1 tsp cumin seeds
1 tsp coriander seeds
1 tsp mustard seeds
6 cloves
40g butter or ghee
2 onions, finely chopped
3 garlic cloves, crushed
thumb-sized piece of fresh ginger,
  peeled and grated
1 tsp ground turmeric

1 tsp garam masala
1 x 400g tin plum tomatoes
2 tsp curry leaves
salt and black pepper

For the cecina
150g gram (chickpea) flour
½ stock cube dissolved in 225ml
  boiling water
2 tbsp extra-virgin olive oil

To serve
4 tbsp natural yoghurt
small bunch of fresh coriander, chopped
2 spring onions, sliced

Pop the potatoes into a pan of cold, salted water. Bring to the boil, then lower the heat to medium and simmer for 10 minutes. Drain, keeping about a mugful of the starchy water, and set aside.

While the potatoes are boiling, toast the cumin, coriander and mustard seeds in a dry frying pan over a low heat for a couple of minutes until fragrant. Transfer to a mortar along with the cloves and use the pestle to grind to a powder.

Warm the butter or ghee in a casserole dish over a low to medium heat and add the onions. Cook for 5 minutes, then add the ground spices, followed by the garlic, ginger, turmeric and garam masala. Mix well, then cook for a further 5 minutes.

Chop the cooked potatoes into chunks (crumbly bits are fine as they will thicken your curry) and pour into the spicy onions. Stir, then add in the tinned tomatoes, crushing them with your hands as they fall in.

(continued overleaf)

Add the reserved starchy water along with the curry leaves and plenty of salt and pepper. Cover the pan and leave to simmer for 10 minutes, then remove the lid and simmer for a further 5–10 minutes while you make the cecina.

Sift the flour into a bowl, add the vegetable stock and whisk until there are no more lumps; set aside.

Place a non-stick pan over a medium–high heat and add 1/2 tablespoon of oil. When hot, pour in a ladleful of the batter. Tilt the pan to spread evenly, and use a spatula to push the sides of the batter down a little. After about a minute, when bubbles form, slide the spatula around and under the pancake, then give the pan a shake to move it around. Flip it like the pro pancaker you are, and cook the other side for a further minute or so before setting on a plate. Repeat to make the remaining pancakes.

Ladle the curry into bowls and top with a spoonful of yoghurt, some chopped coriander and sliced spring onion. Serve with the pancakes.

Sweet Potato and Feta Salad

This is a good dish for wintry brunches – it's delicious with boiled eggs, prosciutto and Bloody Marys... It's also lovely at room temperature, so don't panic too much about timings, but if you do decide to prepare this a little ahead, toss everything together only at the last minute.

Preparation time: 10 minutes
Cooking time: 30 minutes
Serves: 4

3 sweet potatoes
3 garlic cloves
3 bay leaves

2 tbsp olive oil, plus extra for drizzling
200g kale
½ tbsp rapeseed or other neutral oil
200g good-quality feta cheese
1½ tbsp cider vinegar
salt and black pepper

Preheat the oven to 180°C/gas 4.

Wash the sweet potatoes and slice off any gnarly bits. Chop into 2cm squares and place on a baking tray. Add the whole garlic cloves and bay leaves. Spoon over the olive oil, then sprinkle over some salt and pepper. Roast in the oven for 30 minutes, tossing every so often, until the sweet potato skin is crispy and the flesh is soft.

Meanwhile, if you purchased an un-chopped bunch of kale, pick the leaves from their tough stems. Otherwise, empty the bag of chopped kale onto another large baking tray. Drizzle over the rapeseed oil and mix as best as you can to ensure an even coverage (be less sparing and more daring than us with the oil if you wish, we're just trying to behave). Bake for 8–10 minutes, or until crispy. Don't panic if some bits go brown: it's all good, as Gwynnie would say.

When the kale and sweet potato are both ready, toss together in a large serving bowl. Crumble in the feta, sprinkle over the cider vinegar and add an extra drizzle of olive oil. Check the seasoning, then you're good to go.

Mexican Scrambled Egg Tacos

These scrambled eggs are a meal in themselves but are especially good – and go a lot further – when spooned into small tortillas and garnished with avocado, coriander, hot sauce and even a little cheese, if you fancy.

It used to be hard to get corn tortillas in the UK, but Cool Chile Co make wonderful ones that you can order online and freeze, if necessary. They have a different flavour and texture from wheat tortillas, and are also gluten-free, making this a good brunch option for coeliacs, who can feel left out as everyone digs into round after round of hot toast.

We allow for three tacos per person, or two if you are going to serve these alongside something else (the home fries on page 188 are a good option).

Preparation time: 10 minutes
Cooking time: 15 minutes
Serves: 4–6

1½ onions (300g), very finely chopped
10 small tomatoes (500g), finely chopped
3 serrano or jalepeño chillies, thinly sliced
small bunch of coriander, half finely
   chopped, leaves picked from the
   other half

12 eggs
2 avocados, halved and stoned
1 lime, juice of
2 tbsp neutral oil
12 corn tortillas (15cm in diameter)
   or wheat tortillas
salt
chilli sauce, to serve

Prepare all the ingredients that need chopping. Whisk the eggs together in a large bowl.

Slice the avocado halves while still in their skins, then scoop the slices out with a spoon. Put on a plate, squeeze over the lime juice and sprinkle with some salt.

Add the oil to a pan over a medium heat. Cook the onions with a pinch of salt until soft but not brown (around 3–4 minutes), then add the tomatoes and chillies and cook for another 5 minutes. It shouldn't be watery – you want a paste-like consistency.

Turn the heat down ever so slightly (not low, but the lowest end of medium). Pour the eggs into the pan and add a pinch of salt and the chopped coriander. Using a wooden spoon, stir fairly continuously, scraping the bottom of the pan, until you achieve a good scrambled egg consistency. Remove from the heat slightly earlier than you think wise – the eggs will continue to cook.

Warm the tortillas briefly in a dry frying pan over a low to medium heat, then serve immediately with the eggs, sliced avocado, coriander leaves and chilli sauce.

Breakfast Burritos

If you have sausage FOMO – and what meat-eating breakfaster hasn't experienced this at some point – just add some chopped chorizo to the beans. You want chunkier, firmer than normal scrambled eggs with large curds here, or your burrito will be too sloppy.

Preparation time: 10 minutes
Cooking time: 15–20 minutes
Serves: 4

2 avocados
juice of 1 lime
salt
10 eggs
1 tbsp oil
150g Cheddar, grated
4 tortilla wraps
hot sauce, to serve

For the coriander beans
2 tbsp oil
1 onion, chopped
salt
1 medium bunch of coriander
   (around 40g), finely chopped
2 x 400g tins pinto beans in water
¼ tsp chipotle chilli powder

To cook the beans, add the oil to a pan and put over a medium heat. Add the onion and a pinch of salt and fry for around 5 minutes until starting to colour. Add the coriander and fry for a couple of minutes, then pour in the beans and a little of their liquid, and chipotle and cook for another 10 minutes or so, stirring occasionally with a wooden spoon and adding a little splash of water if it looks like it's really drying out. It shouldn't be saucy or you'll have a soggy burrito. Taste for seasoning, adjusting as necessary, and keep warm over a very low heat.

Halve the avocados and scoop their flesh out into another bowl. Squeeze over lime juice and salt to taste and mix together loosely so it's still chunky.

Whisk the eggs together. Add the oil to a pan over a medium to low heat. Pour in the eggs. Leave for 30 seconds to a minute, until they start to cook around the edges, then sprinkle over the cheese. When the cheese has melted slightly, scrape the eggs from the sides of the pan using a silicone spatula or wooden spoon. Fold and flip the egg curds occasionally, taking care not to break them up too much, until just cooked through. Season and remove from the heat.

Warm the tortillas in a hot pan for 20 seconds on each side then transfer to plates. Add the filling to the middle of the tortilla: spoon on beans, eggs and avocado then top with hot sauce. Wrap up tightly: fold the top and bottom in over the filling, then fold both left and right sides over to cover. Slice in half with a sharp knife and eat immediately.

Quesadilla'd Huevos Rancheros

A happy marriage of two of the greatest Mexican inventions: Quesadillas and Huevos Rancheros. The trick is to cook your bottom tortilla slowly and wait for the egg to go opaque. A firm, slightly crispy base and a semi-cooked egg will make it easier to flip without any drama.

Preparation time: 5 minutes
Cooking time: 20 minutes
Serves: 2

4 small soft flour tortillas
2 eggs
1 tbsp Greek yoghurt
small handful of coriander leaves, to garnish

For the ranchero filling
2 tbsp olive oil
½ red onion, finely chopped
1 garlic clove, finely chopped
1 yellow pepper, deseeded and chopped

1 heaped tbsp tomato purée
½ tsp ground cumin
½ tsp smoked paprika
1 x 400g tin black beans or kidney beans
125g ricotta cheese
handful of baby leaf spinach
squeeze of lime juice (optional)
salt and black pepper

For the salsa
2 tomatoes
1 avocado
juice of ½ lime

First attend to the ranchero filing: put a tablespoon of the olive oil in a frying pan and place over a medium to low heat. Add the red onion and garlic and cook gently for a few minutes. Once the onions have softened, add the chopped yellow pepper. Follow with the tomato purée, the remaining olive oil, some seasoning and the cumin and paprika. Stir together, adding a splash of water if you need to, then add the beans and ricotta.

Stir and heat through mashing some of the beans with a wooden spoon as you go and adding a splash of water if needed. Now add the spinach, followed by a squeeze of lime or some more water. Keep stirring to coat the spinach in the hot beans and, once the leaves have wilted, you're ready to prepare your salsa.

Finely chop the tomatoes and place in a bowl. Peel and stone the avocado and chop the flesh into small dice. Add to the tomatoes, squeeze over the lime juice and season to taste.

Now it's time to assemble the first quesadilla. Place a non-stick frying pan over a medium heat and pop a tortilla straight in. Once the tortilla feels hot to the touch, crack an egg on it. Lift and tilt the pan to distribute the egg white as thinly as possible. After a minute or two (once the

(continued overleaf)

egg begins to turn opaque), spoon and smooth the bean mixture over the tortilla, avoiding the yolk. Season. Wait another minute before placing a second tortilla over the top. Press down lightly then slide a spatula under the bottom tortilla.

Carefully flip it (use a plate if helpful) and cook for another couple of minutes until golden – lift it from time to time with the spatula to check.

Slide the quesadilla onto a plate and cut into quarters using a pair of scissors. Top with a few spoonfuls of the salsa and some yoghurt, followed by a sprinkling of coriander. Serve to the lucky recipient while you repeat to make your own quesadilla.

Spiced Potato Cakes with Watercress and Quail Egg Salad

We think this provides the perfect amount of potato cake per person, but if you want to bulk it up a bit, you could add some steamed or chargrilled asparagus to the salad.

Preparation time: 15 minutes
Cooking time: 25 minutes
Serves: 4

450g potatoes, peeled and
  roughly chopped
3 tbsp plain flour
1 egg
½ tsp cayenne pepper
sprinkle of dried chilli flakes
1 spring onion
2 tbsp sunflower oil
salt and black pepper

For the salad
12 quail eggs
½ tbsp sesame oil
½ tbsp olive oil
1 tsp rice wine vinegar
80g watercress
2 tbsp snipped cress
8 radishes, thinly sliced

Place the potatoes in a pan of cold, salted water. Bring to the boil and simmer for 10 minutes, or until tender. Drain, then mash in the pan you used to cook them in. Add the flour, egg, cayenne pepper, chilli flakes and seasoning, then snip in the spring onion using kitchen scissors. Mix well.

Now prepare your salad: bring a small pan of water to the boil, add the quail eggs and cook for 2 minutes. Drain and hold under cold running water until cool enough to handle, then peel, halve and set aside. Put the oil and vinegar in the bottom of a salad bowl, then top with the watercress and cress. Add the sliced radishes.

Time to fry the potato cakes. Preheat the oven to 140°C/gas 1. Place a frying pan over a medium heat and add half the oil: you want it hot but not smoking so keep a close eye on it. Once the pan is ready, add 3 or 4 heaped teaspoon-sized dollops of the potato mix, resisting the temptation to flatten them just yet. Wait for a minute or so, then, using a spatula, flip them over. Now use the spatula to flatten the cakes as much as you can and leave to cook for a minute or two until golden. Flip the cakes over one last time and cook the squidged-out edges of the first side.

Once the first batch of cakes is done, place in the oven to keep warm. Add a little more sunflower oil to the pan and continue making potato cakes until you have used up all the mixture.

When you're ready to serve, toss the salad. Pop a few potato cakes on each plate, add some salad and finish with the quail egg halves. Enjoy!

Mediterranean Salad with Quick Caponata and Goats' Cheese Toasts

This is one of those dishes that people can just keep coming back for – make sure you place any leftover caponata, toasts and salad on the table so that your guests can enjoy seconds or even thirds.

Preparation time: 15 minutes
Cooking time: 40 minutes
Serves: 4

1 head of lettuce, leaves separated
1 cantaloupe melon
400g prosciutto
1 baguette, cut into 1cm slices
　　on the diagonal
1 garlic clove, halved
olive oil, for drizzling
150g soft goats' cheese
2 tsp dried thyme

For the quick caponata
350g cherry tomatoes, halved
3 aubergines, cut into 3cm chunks
100g Kalamata olives
4 tbsp olive oil
salt and black pepper

For the salad dressing
1 tbsp olive oil
2 tsp red wine vinegar
2 tsp Dijon mustard

First make the quick(er) caponata: preheat the oven to 180°C/gas 4. Place the cherry tomato halves in a bowl, sprinkle with salt and set aside. Place the aubergine chunks in two ovenproof dishes (you don't want them to be overcrowded), drizzle over some olive oil and season with salt and pepper. Bake in the oven for 10 minutes, then divide the tomatoes and olives between the two dishes, adding some more olive oil if needed, and return to the oven for a further 25 minutes. Use a metal spatula to scrape the vegetables from the bottom of the dishes from time to time and turn them over for even cooking and to prevent any sticking.

Once the aubergines are golden brown and the cherry tomatoes are oozing and juicy,

place in a serving bowl and mix together to combine all the flavours.

Meanwhile, combine the dressing ingredients in the bottom of a salad bowl, add salt and pepper and top with the salad leaves. Halve the melon using a sharp knife and scoop out the seeds. Slice into wedges, then remove the skin by sliding the knife under the flesh along the curve. (This could also be done ahead of time and the melon kept in the fridge – just make sure you bring it to room temperature before eating). Distribute the melon between 4 plates along with the prosciutto.

When the caponata is almost ready, lightly toast the baguette slices (allow for three

(continued overleaf)

tartines per person), either under the grill or in your toaster in batches. Rub a halved garlic clove over both sides and drizzle over a little olive oil.

Arrange the toasts on a baking tray and spread the goats' cheese on them. Add a sprinkling of thyme and a final drizzle of olive oil. Bake for 5 minutes until the cheese has melted and is a little brown in places.

Add the hot toasts to the plates of melon and prosciutto and bring everything else to the table, allowing your guests to help themselves to salad and caponata.

American-style Biscuits

Akin to a scone, these cheesy American-style 'biscuits' are delicious sliced in half, and smothered with butter. Enjoy with bacon and eggs or sliced avocado. They will keep for a few days in a sealed tin, and are best lightly toasted after day one.

Preparation time: 10 minutes
Cooking time: 10 minutes
Makes: 8 biscuits

200g self-raising flour
1 tsp baking powder

40g butter, cut into cubes
pinch of salt
25g grated Parmesan cheese
½ tsp finely chopped rosemary
1 egg, beaten
25ml milk, plus extra for brushing

Preheat the oven to 200°C/gas 6 and lightly grease a baking tray.

Sift the flour and baking powder into a large mixing bowl and add the butter. Use the tips of your fingers to rub the butter and flour together and create a breadcrumb texture. Add the salt, chopped rosemary and Parmesan and mix well. Stir in the egg and milk and use your hands to form a dough.

Knead lightly, then turn the dough onto a lightly floured surface. Continue kneading for a further minute, then roll out the dough to a 1cm thickness. Use a round 5cm cutter to stamp out the biscuits, then place on the greased baking tray. Brush the tops with milk and bake in the oven for 10 minutes, or until risen and golden.

Roasted Tomato, Spring Onion and Bacon Quiche

Roasting the tomatoes concentrates their flavour and stops the quiche from being watery, while the spring onions become deliciously sweet. Many people think cheese in a quiche is gilding the lily; we do not fall into this group.

Of course you don't have to make your own pastry – your quiche will still be delicious if you use ready-made. If you do make your

own, you can prepare all the components in advance up to the final bake: just cover the blind baked pastry with cling film when cool and leave at room temperature, cover and chill the separate cooked filling ingredients, then assemble everything half an hour or so before you want to eat. Some crisp little gem leaves with a mustardy dressing are all you need alongside.

Preparation time: 30–40 minutes,
   (plus chilling if making your own pastry)
Cooking time: 1½ hours
Serves: 4–6

300g baby plum tomatoes, halved
2 tbsp olive oil, plus a little extra
leaves from 3 sprigs of thyme
   or 1 tsp dried thyme
2 bunches of spring onions
   (around 300g), trimmed
8 rashers smoked streaky bacon,
   finely chopped into strips
4 eggs

180ml double cream
100g crème fraîche
40g Cheddar cheese, grated
salt and black pepper
2 tbsp snipped cress
8 radishes, thinly sliced

For the pastry
270g plain flour
good pinch of salt
135g cold butter, chopped into
   very small cubes
3–4 tbsp very cold water
1 beaten egg, for brushing

Preheat the oven to 180°C/gas 4. Grease a 25cm loose-bottomed tart tin (a scrap ripped off the butter wrapper is handy for this) and line two baking trays with foil.

First make the pastry. Add the flour and salt to a bowl and whisk together. Add the butter and rub it into the flour with your fingertips (or you can use a food processor for this bit). When it has a crumbly sort of

texture mix in the first tablespoon of water. Keep adding the water until the pastry comes together into a ball. Wrap in cling film and chill in the fridge for at least 30 minutes.

Place the halved tomatoes on one of the lined baking trays, drizzle with a tablespoon of the oil, season with salt and pepper and sprinkle over the thyme leaves. Add the spring onions to the other lined tray, drizzle

(continued overleaf)

over the remaining tablespoon of oil and season with salt and pepper. Roast the tomatoes and spring onions for 30 minutes, until the tomatoes are shrunken and the onions are a bit browned. Snip or cut the onions into little pieces, discarding any very crisp green end bits. Meanwhile fry the bacon in a little oil until crispy.

Place a large piece of baking paper on your work surface and sprinkle a little flour on it, add the pastry, sprinkle a little more flour over, then cover with another piece of baking paper. This makes rolling easier and saves you wiping down your kitchen counter. Roll the pastry out between the paper until large enough to line the prepared tin with about a 5cm overhang.

Carefully lift the pastry into the tin, pushing it firmly into the bottom and up over the sides (remember that it will shrink). Use any scraggly extra bits to bolster the sides or patch up anything that's gone awry. If the pastry seems a bit warm by this point, pop it back in the fridge for 10 minutes before continuing. Prick the pastry base with a fork, line with baking paper and fill with baking beans or dried beans. Blind bake for 20 minutes, then remove the paper and beans, brush the pastry with the whisked egg, and bake for another 15–20 minutes until golden brown.

Your oven will probably cook unevenly, so keep an eye on how the pastry is colouring and rotate the tin if necessary. Remove from the oven and leave on a wire rack to cool.

To make the filling, whisk the eggs in a bowl, then beat in the cream and crème fraîche until slightly frothy. If you are making the filling in advance, cover and put it in the fridge at this point. When you are ready to fill the quiche case, season and whisk again.

Turn the oven temperature down to 170°C/ gas 3. Add the tomatoes and spring onions to the pastry case, then scatter the bacon and cheese over them. Carefully pour in the creamy egg mixture. Add any excess bacon fat from the pan and any roasted tomato juice, giving it a little swirl to distribute.

Bake for around 30–35 minutes – again rotating the tin so that the pastry and filling colour evenly – until the top is puffy and golden in places. Steel yourself and leave to cool until slightly warm, then slice and serve. Any leftovers (one can dream) will keep until the next day, wrapped in cling film and kept in the fridge – just reheat in the oven or microwave.

All-day Breakfast Potstickers

A traditional dim sum brunch generally consists of lots of different delicious bite-sized things that you select from a series of stacked basket trays, most of which take a great deal of skill and practice to make well. These part-fried, part-steamed potstickers (fried and steamed dumplings) combine mainstays of the all-day breakfast (sausage and egg) with spicy kimchi, spring onion and ginger. They are in no way authentic but they are easy enough to construct, even if your last experience of pleating was a paper fan you made in Year 5.

We think it's worth making the quantity below as, when it comes to dumplings, more is definitely more. Once you get going, it's pretty absorbing (in the way repetitive tasks that you don't do very often can be) – but you can halve the number if you want.

Preparation time: 45 minutes
Cooking time: 20 minutes
Serves: 4–6 (makes 40 dumplings)

40 ready-made dumpling wrappers
   (2 packets)
4 eggs, beaten
knob of butter
150g kimchi, chopped
3 spring onions, sliced
finger-sized piece of fresh ginger
   (around 15g), peeled and finely grated

400g sausage meat, squeezed out
   of 6 sausages
flour, for dusting
1 tbsp neutral cooking oil
100–120ml water, plus extra for the
   flour paste
salt and black pepper

For the dipping sauce
3 tbsp Chinkiang black rice vinegar
2 tsp chilli oil
squirt of ketchup (optional)

Take the dumpling wrappers out of the fridge and allow to come up to room temperature. Meanwhile, season the beaten eggs. Melt the butter in a small pan over a medium to low heat. Pour in the eggs and stir fairly continuously with a wooden spoon, scraping the pan, until you achieve a good scrambled egg consistency. Take off the heat.

Place the chopped kimchi, spring onions, ginger and sausage meat in a large bowl and mix together. When the eggs are cool, fold them in too.

Mix together a little flour and some water in a small bowl to make a paste for sealing the dumplings.

Place a teaspoonful of sausage-egg mix in the middle of a dumpling wrapper. As with crispy duck pancakes, it is tempting to overstuff them, but try to resist as this makes them harder to close. Dab around the top half of the wrapper with the flour paste, then bring the bottom half up and pinch together in the middle with your thumb and index finger. Starting from the

(continued overleaf)

right, fold the closest half over itself and towards the pinched-together middle; repeat until one side of the dumpling is pleated, then squeeze together to seal. Repeat with the left-hand side. Pleating takes a little bit of getting used to but it should get easier with practice. This method is the one we find easiest, but if you find a way that works better for you, go with it! Line up the finished dumplings on a lightly floured tray.

Add the oil to a large sauté or frying pan for which you have a lid, and put over a medium to high heat. When hot – but not smoking – add the dumplings, flat side down, pleated size up. Lower the heat to medium and fry for around 5 minutes – you want the bottoms to go golden brown and crisp, not to burn. At this point, add the measured water and cover the pan quickly to trap the steam. Cook for 15 minutes, adding a splash more water if you think it's needed, until the dumplings have finished cooking through.

Mix the dipping sauce ingredients in a small bowl and serve with the cooked dumplings.

Tartines, Toasties and Sandwiches

Sabich

If you take care with the seasoning and preparation of each component, what you will end up with is so, so much more than the sum of its parts: a Jerusalem breakfast of dreams.

The aubergine, salad and sauces can all be prepared in advance but the sandwich should definitely be assembled at the last minute, with freshly boiled eggs and deliciously warm pitta.

Preparation time: 25 minutes
Cooking time: 20 minutes
Serves: 4

6 tbsp olive oil
3 aubergines, thinly sliced into rounds
4 eggs
4 pitta breads

For the salad
½ cucumber, diced
4–5 tomatoes, diced
1 red onion, finely chopped
handful of fresh dill, finely chopped

generous handful of fresh parsley,
    finely chopped
drizzle of olive oil
salt and black pepper

For the tahini sauce
5 tbsp tahini
juice of 1 lemon

For the curried yoghurt
5 tbsp Greek yoghurt or labneh
1 garlic clove, crushed
1 tsp curry powder
½ tsp turmeric

Drizzle 2 tablespoons of the oil into a frying over a medium heat and, once hot, add the aubergine slices in batches. Cook for a few minutes until golden brown on both sides, using tongs to turn them halfway. Add more oil as and when you need it.

To make the salad, put all the ingredients into a bowl. Mix to combine and season with salt and pepper.

To make the sauce: spoon the tahini into a bowl, add the lemon juice and a few tablespoons of tepid water, mixing as you go until you have a fairly wet but creamy consistency. Taste to check the seasoning.

To make the curried yoghurt: place the yoghurt in a bowl and add the garlic, spices and some salt and pepper. Taste to check the seasoning.

About 10 minutes before you are about to serve, preheat the oven to 180°C/gas 4. Bring a pan of water to the boil, add the eggs and cook for 7½ minutes. Run them under the cold tap for a moment so they are cool enough to handle, then peel and slice.

Place the pittas in the oven and cook until they are warmed through (you want to be able to open and stuff them without any cracking). Once ready, halve them and,

(continued overleaf)

taking once piece at a time, open the pocket. Add a dollop of tahini, a dollop of yoghurt and a spoonful of salad. Follow with a generous stuffing of aubergine, then some sliced egg. Use a fork to cram it in and seriously, don't worry about overfilling. It's a sight to behold: generous of spirit, and you can always give people kitchen paper to mop up any chin drippage. No one is judging. Follow with a dollop more of tahini and curried yoghurt and finish with another spoonful of salad. Hand to someone immediately to enjoy.

Leek and Taleggio Tartine

A classic combination of flavours on toast, and – frankly – lovely at any time of day.

Preparation time: 2 minutes
Cooking time: 20 minutes
Serves: 2

1 tbsp olive oil
knob of butter
1 medium leek
2 large slices of good bread
200g taleggio cheese
salt and black pepper

Heat the olive oil and butter in a frying pan over a medium heat while you trim, wash and slice the leek into rounds. Add the leek slices to the pan, then fry relatively slowly for 15 minutes until silky and translucent, stirring occasionally to stop them catching.

Preheat the grill to high while you lightly toast the bread and slice the taleggio, discarding any thick rind. Place the toast on a baking tray, topped with the slices of taleggio. Grill for a few minutes until the cheese has melted, then remove and top the tartines with the leek, shared equally between the two slices. Add salt and black pepper, then place under the grill for a further minute. Serve immediately.

Fresh Bruschette

The quantities here allow for approximately two slices of each topping combination per person, but if you want to keep things simpler and cheaper, just stick to a couple of combinations and increase the relative quantities.

Conversely, if you want to make a meal of it, add some homemade pesto, sliced boiled eggs and caponata (see page 58) to the mix.

If you're making the peach bruschette, do them last lest they make the bread soggy.

Preparation time: 10 minutes
Serves: 4

2 good-quality fresh baguettes
500g ricotta cheese

To serve
grated lemon zest

For the toppings
2 peaches, sliced, plus 90g Parma ham
50g strawberries, sliced, plus 1 tbsp basil
    leaves, finely chopped
1 banana, thinly sliced, plus 1 tbsp chopped
    salted peanuts
50g cucumber, thinly sliced, plus 1 tbsp
    fresh tarragon, finely chopped
salt and black pepper

Slice the baguette into thin (1.5cm) slices on the diagonal, then lightly toast on both sides under the grill. Allow to cool, then spread ricotta on all of the slices.

Add your chosen toppings to the toasts and lay them out on a platter. Finish with a grating of lemon zest and black pepper and a sprinkling of salt, where necessary.

Avocado Toast

We hesitated to include this as it can hardly be called a recipe but, at the same time, no breakfast or brunch menu is complete without it these days. Also, there are few things that you can make in mere seconds that are as satisfying – for this reason we eat it pretty much every day.

We most often jazz up our avo with lemon, salt and chilli, but lime is great for bringing it to life too, as are paprika, cayenne, za'atar, dukkah or any number of other sprinklable toppings. By all means slice your avocado if your aesthetic tastes recoil from squishing it, but we draw the line at sculpting it into a rose.

Preparation time: 2 minutes max
Serves: 1

1 large slice of sourdough or other bread
½ perfectly ripe avocado
good squeeze of lemon juice
pinch of sea salt
pinch of chilli flakes

Toast your bread. Use a teaspoon to scoop the avocado out of its skin in small rounds and squish these down onto the toast with a fork. Squeeze over the lemon juice and sprinkle with salt and chilli. Eat immediately.

Sausage and Egg Muffin

If you're going to pay homage to the ultimate fast food breakfast sandwich, it is essential that you have a perfectly round, compact egg to snuggle into your muffin. The uniformity of the egg just makes it: we don't know why – nostalgia maybe? To achieve this eggy holy grail, we use a poachette ring; this is basically a muffin or crumpet ring but with a ridiculous name. If you have a muffin or crumpet ring, use that, or an appropriately sized biscuit cutter. For a DIY ring, use a cleaned out tin of tuna (with top and bottom removed) – just grease it well and be careful handling the sharp edges.

Preparation time: 5 minutes
Cooking time: 10 minutes
Serves: Makes 4

4 good-quality sausages
  (around 100g each)
1 tsp crushed fennel seeds (optional)
1 tbsp neutral oil, plus a little extra
  for the eggs

4 English muffins (see page 185 or
  use shop-bought)
butter, for spreading
4 slices of Monterey Jack or other cheese
4 eggs
salt and black pepper
condiments of your choice, to serve

Slit the sausages open and squeeze the meat into a bowl. Season with a little salt and pepper and the fennel seeds (if using) and mix together. Form into four equal-sized patties – slightly larger in diameter than your muffins (they will shrink a bit when cooked).

Add the oil to a large frying pan over a medium heat. When hot, add the patties and fry until cooked through and nicely browned (around 2 minutes on each side).

Split the muffins – traditionally you're meant to pull them apart but we admit to often using a knife – and toast lightly. Butter and leave to sit on a greaseproof lined baking tray. Place a slice of cheese and a sausage patty on half the muffins. Preheat the oven to 200°C/gas 6.

Lightly grease your poachettes or biscuit cutters, then add a little oil to a large non-stick frying pan over a medium heat. Place the poachettes/rings in the pan. Crack the eggs into them and cook for around 2½ minutes. Remove the ring, flip the eggs with a spatula and cook for 30 more seconds. Place an egg on each sausage patty, topping with a plain muffin half. Warm through in the oven for a couple of minutes or until the cheese has melted. Eat immediately with your sauce(s) of choice.

Chilli Cheese Toast

This Anglo-Indian classic is given a refreshing
lift by the addition of zesty herb chutney.
You could, of course, make it into a toastie
instead, or top with a fried egg.

Preparation time: 2 minutes
Cooking time: 20 minutes
Serves: 2 (makes 4 slices)

200g Cheddar cheese, grated
4 green chillies, deseeded and
   finely chopped
½ red onion, finely chopped
pinch of chilli powder
4 slices of sourdough or other bread

For the chutney
¼ red onion
3cm piece of fresh ginger, peeled
30g coriander
30g mint
¼ tsp ground turmeric
¼ tsp garam masala
pinch of sugar
pinch of salt
juice of 1 lime

Mix the Cheddar, chillies, onion and chilli
powder together in a bowl until combined.

To make the chutney, place all the
ingredients in a food processor or blender
and pulse until smooth and sauce-like.
Adjust the salt, sugar and lime juice to taste.
Transfer to a serving bowl.

Preheat the grill, then lightly toast
your bread. Spread the cheese mixture
evenly on to the toasted bread slices – there
should be enough to be generous. Cheese
on toast is not the time to scrimp. Grill for
4–5 minutes, until melted and crisp and
brown in places. Slice and eat immediately
with a dollop of the chutney.

Asparagus, Romesco and Egg on Toast

This is the kind of vegetarian meal that has carnivores looking longingly from their bacon sarnies. The asparagus season is a glorious but brief time: if you can't get hold of any, spring onions are a classic accompaniment to romesco and you don't need to blanch them: just whack them on the griddle pan and cook until charred and sweet inside. We like this with soft-boiled eggs but you could of course have fried or even poached if you're feeling ambitious.

Preparation time: 5 minutes
Cooking time: 10 minutes
Serves: 4

2 bunches of asparagus, woody
   ends discarded
4 eggs
olive oil, to serve
4 generous slices of sourdough
   or other bread
salt and black pepper

For the romesco (makes 1 x 450g jar)
40g blanched almonds, toasted
40g blanched hazelnuts, toasted
1 x 350g jar roasted red peppers
   and a little of their juice
3 tbsp olive oil
2 tbsp sherry vinegar
pinch of salt
½ tsp smoked paprika
½ tsp cayenne pepper
pinch of chilli flakes
2–4 garlic cloves
1 chunky slice of slightly stale sourdough

Put all the romesco ingredients into a food processor and blend to a pesto-like consistency.

Cook the asparagus in a pan of lightly salted boiling water until just tender – for about 2 minutes. Using tongs or a slotted spoon, transfer immediately to a bowl of cold water (drain and top up if it gets a bit warm).

Put the eggs in a separate pan of boiling water and cook for 6 minutes. Hold them under running cold water until cool enough to handle, then peel. Add to the bowl of asparagus (changing the water again if necessary).

Place a griddle pan over a medium heat. Dry the asparagus on kitchen paper, then rub in a little bit of olive oil. Lay the asparagus in the pan and cook until you get those nice char marks, turning every so often.

Toast the bread and top with the asparagus. Pat the eggs dry, then slice in half and place on top of the asparagus. Season with salt and pepper, then spoon over the romesco. Eat immediately.

Cheese and Spring Onion Toastie

Whenever we see grated Gruyère in the shops, we pounce on it. It's delicious sprinkled on pasta, homemade pizza and, of course, perfect for an added cheesy oomph in toasties.

Toasties are surprisingly delicious with jam, the sweetness complementing the salty cheese. Try this one with the sour cherry compote on page 167, and perhaps alongside some lightly dressed lamb's lettuce.

Preparation time: 2 minutes
Cooking time: 2 minutes
Serves: 2

2 large slices of sourdough bread
15g butter
80g Cheddar cheese
1 spring onion, finely chopped
2 tbsp grated Gruyère cheese
dash of Worcestershire sauce (optional)

Preheat your grill to high and lightly toast the bread. Remove from the grill and butter both sides of each slice.

Finely slice the Cheddar and place on the toast. Distribute the chopped spring onion between the slices. Finish with a sprinkling of Gruyère and a dash of Worcestershire sauce, if using. Place under the grill for a few minutes, until bubbling and golden brown. Eat immediately.

BLT Buffet Bar

Whether you are making sandwiches for two or a few, there is something about serving the individual ingredients on big platters that we find particularly conducive to brunch time. You can prepare things ahead, yes, but there's also something languorous and indulgent about it. It feels generous – you can help yourself, you can have seconds! – but there's also an implicit agreement that everyone around the table is going to take time and pleasure in the meal, spreading the mayo and arranging the bacon on their bread just so.

Allow four rashers of streaky bacon or three rashers of back bacon and half a large tomato per sandwich.

Order of service

- Mayo is a must; whether you make it yourself (see page 194) or scoop it out of a jar, make sure it's to hand.
- Fill up your pepper grinder: freshly ground pepper is key to a good BLT.
- Plunge your lettuce (large, crisp-leafed: this is no place for spinach or rocket) into ice-cold water, then spin it or give it a good shake outside. Keep the leaves wrapped in damp kitchen paper in the fridge until you're ready to lay everything out.
- Buy the ripest, juiciest tomatoes you can find (give them a sniff) and don't let them near your fridge. You cannot make a great BLT without a good tomato. Slice them into generous rounds, arrange on a large plate or platter and sprinkle with a little sea salt.
- Fifteen minutes before you want to eat, grill your bacon until super crispy: if you can snap it in half, so much the better (streaky bacon is especially good for this).
- There is no bread that can sully a BLT, so use whatever type you like. If it's sliced, toast it lightly – it doesn't need to be served hot, so you can start this while the bacon is grilling.

4

Quick Ideas for One or Two

Poached Eggs with Yoghurt and Chilli Butter

This is our version of the classic Turkish dish çilbir. You probably have most of the ingredients knocking around your cupboard and fridge, so it's especially good for those times when you hadn't planned on cooking anything but feel too lazy to throw a coat on over your PJs and nip out to the shops (if nipping out is an option).

Preparation time: 3 minutes
Cooking time: 2 minutes
Serves: 2

200g Greek yoghurt
½ garlic clove, crushed
40g unsalted butter

½–1 tsp chilli flakes (depending how spicy they are)
½ tsp cayenne pepper
½ tsp paprika (hot or smoked)
¼ tsp ground cumin
4 eggs
bread, for toasting

With a spoon, beat together the yoghurt and garlic until smooth. Spoon into two small bowls.

In a pan over a low heat, melt the butter with the chilli and spices, taking care not to let it burn, until it is red and infused.

Poach the eggs for 1½ minutes (see page 14), then remove with a slotted spoon and drain on kitchen paper. Pop the bread into the toaster while the eggs are in the pan.

Place a poached egg on top of the yoghurt and pour over the chilli butter. Serve with toast for mopping up all the yolk, yoghurt and spicy butter.

Green Scrambled Eggs

This will give you all the fresh flavours of
a Thai escape without the expense.

Preparation time: 10 minutes
Cooking time: 5 minutes
Serves: 2

1 medium bunch of coriander
1 tbsp mint leaves
1 tbsp Greek yoghurt
thumb-sized piece of fresh ginger, peeled
thumb-sized piece of lemongrass
1 green bird's-eye chilli, deseeded

drizzle of extra-virgin olive oil
zest and juice of ½ lime
6 eggs
splash of fish sauce
splash of soy sauce
splash of teriyaki sauce
½ tsp sugar
generous knob of butter
pinch of salt and black pepper
toast, to serve

Add the coriander, stalks and all, to a blender
and follow with the mint leaves, yoghurt,
ginger, lemongrass, chilli, lime zest and juice.
Pulse until you have a smooth paste.

Decant the green paste into a large bowl
and crack in the eggs. Add the fish, soy and
teriyaki sauces, followed by the sugar, salt
and pepper. Whisk until combined.

Add the butter to a pan over a medium
to low heat. Once melted, add the green
egg mix. Using a wooden spoon, stir
fairly continuously, scraping the bottom
of the pan as you go, until you achieve a
good scrambled egg consistency: cooked
through, but still creamy.

Pile onto toast and eat immediately.

Menemen

For two years Sophie lived a minute away from a Turkish café called Café Z, and this recipe is a tribute to the hundreds of thousands (approximate figure) of menemen, or Turkish scrambled eggs, she ate in that golden time. This is the basic recipe but you can add any number of extras: crumbled feta, spicy sausage, chopped chilli or wilted spinach (squeeze out any excess liquid) are a few traditional favourites.

Bread for mopping up the last bits of eggy goodness is a must. We recommend the three-ingredient flatbreads (see page 187).

Preparation time: 3 minutes
Cooking time: 15–20 minutes
Serves: 2

1 beef or large ripe tomato, cored and
   flesh chopped
2 tbsp oil (olive or rapeseed)
½ onion, finely chopped
pinch of sea salt
1 long green Turkish pepper, deseeded and
   chopped to a similar size to the tomato
good pinch of chilli flakes (use pul biber
   if you can find it)
knob of butter
4–6 eggs (depending how hungry
   you are), beaten

Put the chopped tomatoes in a colander set over a bowl and leave to drain.

Add the oil to a pan and place over a medium to low heat. When hot, add the onion and sea salt and fry for around 3 minutes, until starting to soften. Add the pepper and cook for another 3 minutes, stirring occasionally.

Increase the heat to medium and stir in the tomatoes and chilli flakes. Cook for 6–7 minutes then taste and adjust the seasoning, adding more chilli and salt as needed.

Add the butter to the pan and, when melted, pour in the eggs. Using a wooden spoon, stir fairly continuously, scraping the pan, until you achieve a good scrambled egg consistency. Finish with an extra sprinkle of chilli, if you like, and serve immediately.

Bircher Muesli

The man behind muesli, Maximilian Bircher-Benner, fed the 'little mush' to patients at his sanitorium in Zurich, adding raw apple, hazelnuts and cream or condensed milk to pre-soaked oats. The apple and oats are kind of mandatory, but anything goes with regard to the other ingredients – use milk or cream and whatever combination of dried fruits and nuts you fancy. We like the slight sourness of dried cherries. Cranberries would work well too. Although the muesli should soak overnight, it takes mere minutes to prepare and can be made in a jar or plastic container, so is great for brunch on the go. In a pinch, you could always soak it first thing in the morning for a few hours.

You can easily multiply the quantities below to serve more than one.

Preparation time: 2 minutes, plus soaking
Serves: 1

30g rolled porridge oats
1 heaped tbsp (20g) dried maraschino
   cherries, roughly chopped
75ml cold water
30ml milk

To serve
1 apple, grated
as much milk as you like – or cream,
   if you're feeling extravagant
dollop of yoghurt (optional)
1 tbsp pistachios and almonds, chopped

Add the oats, cherries, water and milk to a glass jar or plastic container. Cover and leave in the fridge overnight. Grate the apple coarsely. Tip the oat mix into a soup plate or bowl, add three quarters of the apple and mix together a little before adding milk. Top with the yoghurt, if using, and sprinkle over the remaining apple and nuts.

The following three recipes are simpler than those on pages 29–31 in that you pretty much throw ready-made ingredients together and bake them. Easy and perfect for last-minute brunches that need to cater for varied tastes and vegetarians.

Baked eggs with peppers

Preparation time: 2 minutes
Cooking time: 15 minutes
Serves: 2

butter, for greasing
4 eggs
4 heaped tsp soured cream
8 small cooked peppers from a jar
8 sun-dried tomatoes
drizzle of olive oil
pinch of dried thyme
salt and black pepper
buttered toast and chilli sauce, to serve

Preheat the oven to 140°C/gas 1.

Grease two 16cm ovenproof pudding or pie dishes with butter and crack two eggs into each one. If using smaller dishes, such as ramekins, use four and pop an egg into each one. Add equal dollops of soured cream to the respective dishes, then divide the peppers and tomatoes between them, avoiding the yolks. Finish with tiny drizzle of olive oil, a pinch of thyme and some seasoning.

Bake for 15 minutes, or until the whites have set and the yolks are still a bit runny (give the dish a wobble to check). Serve with buttered toast and chilli sauce.

Baked eggs with smoked salmon

Preparation time: 2 minutes
Cooking time: 15 minutes
Serves: 2

butter, for greasing
4 eggs
4 heaped tsp soured cream
140g smoked salmon
1 tbsp fresh dill, chopped
salt and black pepper
buttered toast, to serve

Preheat the oven to 140°C/gas 1.

Grease two 16cm ovenproof pudding or pie dishes with butter and crack two eggs into each one. If using smaller dishes, such as ramekins, use four and pop an egg into each one. Add equal dollops of soured cream to the respective dishes, then divide the smoked salmon between them, avoiding the yolks. Finish with a sprinkling of dill and some seasoning.

Bake for 15 minutes, or until the whites have set and the yolks are still a bit runny (give the dish a wobble to check). Serve with buttered toast.

Baked eggs with chorizo

Preparation time: 2 minutes
Cooking time: 17 minutes
Serves: 2

butter, for greasing
4 eggs
40g chorizo sausage
4 heaped tsp soured cream
1 tsp dried thyme
salt and black pepper
buttered toast, to serve

Preheat the oven to 140°C/gas 1.

Chop the chorizo into chunks and dry-fry it for a few minutes until the fat is starting to run and it is getting a little crispy. Set aside.

Grease two 16cm ovenproof pudding or pie dishes with butter and crack two eggs into each one. If using smaller dishes, such as ramekins, use four and pop an egg into each one. Add equal dollops of soured cream to the respective dishes, then divide the chorizo between them, avoiding the yolks. Finish with a pinch of thyme and some seasoning.

Bake for 15 minutes, or until the whites have set and the yolks are still a bit runny (give the dish a wobble to check). Serve with buttered toast.

Spaghetti Frittata

Although it can be hard to avoid the temptation to eat leftover pasta straight from the pan, this Italian classic is a great way of making it go further. Our leftover pasta of choice is Marcella Hazan's famous three-ingredient sauce with a little spice added: add 2 tins of plum tomatoes to a pan with 2 halved onions and a large knob of butter.

Simmer partially covered for 45–60 minutes until the onions are soft and the sauce is glossy. Season to taste and add a pinch of dried chilli flakes. Roughly cut the onions into bite-sized pieces. Boil 500g spaghetti until al dente and stir into the sauce with a tiny splash of the pasta water. Cook for a minute more, stirring. Try to save some for your frittata…

Preparation time: 10 minutes
Cooking time: 10–15 minutes
Serves: 4

6 eggs
knob of butter
400g leftover tomato pasta, or any
 other pasta
30g Parmesan cheese, grated
salt and black pepper

In a bowl large enough to hold the pasta, whisk the eggs together, then set aside.

Add the butter to a large heavy-based or non-stick frying pan and place over a low to medium heat. Meanwhile, scrape the tomatoey pasta into the bowl of beaten eggs, making sure you get all that good sauce out. Add the Parmesan, then season and mix to combine. Tip the mixture into the buttery pan and cook for 10 minutes or until the eggs are nearly firm. Finish cooking the top for a couple of minutes under a hot grill if you want it to be crispy and browned, or cover the pan with a lid or some foil to allow the steam to finish cooking it.

Leave the frittata to cool slightly before turning onto a plate and slicing into fat wedges. This is lovely with a green salad – either something crisp like little gem, or peppery such as watercress or rocket.

$\textcircled{5}$

Bottomless Brunch

Fried Chicken and Honey Mustard Lettuce Wraps

Fried chicken in the morning is a bit of a spicy meatball, that is to say, a bold move. Like many gloriously indulgent meals, it originates from America, where it would usually be served with waffles and syrup or sandwiched into a Southern-style biscuit (see page 61). Both options are undeniably delicious but we like to make life a bit simpler and serve the chicken with a pile of soft lettuce leaves and a tangy dressing.

Not only does this ensure that the chicken (and no upstart waffle) is the star of the table, but it also makes the meat go a lot further and, crucially, enables you to eat more without feeling like you've beige-binged.

We always opt to shallow-fry, turning the chicken halfway through cooking: this way you have more control, use less oil and don't need any special equipment – just a large sauté pan for which you have a lid (ideally a glass one).

This is a hands-on brunch: tear the chicken with your fingers and add to the middle of a lettuce leaf, drizzle over the spicy sweet sauce, then sprinkle over radishes and chives – and repeat.

The method below owes much to the wisdom of American food writer Laurie Colwin; the dipping sauce is 'borrowed' from Sophie's dad.

Preparation time: 15 minutes, plus chilling
Cooking time: 45 minutes
Serves: 4

1kg free-range chicken pieces (a mixture of breasts and boneless or bone-in thighs and legs)
150ml buttermilk
good squeeze of ketchup
1 tsp salt, plus an extra pinch
200g plain flour
1 tsp paprika (hot or smoked)
½ tsp English mustard powder

about 500ml vegetable oil, for frying (the amount will depend on the size of your pan)

For the honey mustard sauce
100ml buttermilk
2 tbsp English mustard
2 tbsp honey

To serve
1 large soft round lettuce, leaves washed and dried
10 radishes, sliced
small bunch of chives, chopped
hot sauce (optional)

Trim any scraggly bits from the chicken and remove the skin. If using breasts, cut them into two or three roughly equal pieces. Add to a large bowl with the buttermilk, ketchup and pinch of salt. Chill for 2 hours, then place in a cool spot on the counter for

(continued overleaf)

another hour or so, so the meat is not fridge-cold when you fry it. Meanwhile, whisk together the sauce ingredients and keep covered in the fridge.

In a medium bowl, mix together the flour, paprika, teaspoon of salt and mustard powder. Put 2 tablespoons of the flour mixture on a large plate and coat the chicken in it. Keep adding fresh flour mixture as you work to stop everything getting too claggy. Place the floured chicken pieces on a plate or tray.

Preheat the oven to 140°C/gas 1. Line a baking tray with kitchen paper and another with baking paper. Add a good 3cm of oil to a large sauté pan (ideally with a glass lid). Place over a medium to high heat – it's ready when you drop in a little floury ball and it sizzles rapidly.

Carefully add 4–6 pieces of chicken – cook the largest ones first so they can spend

longer in the oven – then cover with the lid and turn the heat down to a low-ish medium. Cook for 6 minutes, then carefully slide the pan over to the next hob, swiftly remove the lid to avoid condensation dripping off it and into the oil. Using tongs, turn the chicken over. As before, cook for another 6 minutes, slide the pan over and take off the lid, then transfer the chicken to the kitchen paper-lined tray. Leave for a minute to drain, then transfer to the other tray and put in the oven. Put the sauté pan, uncovered, back on the heat and allow the oil to come back up to temperature before frying the next batch of chicken in the same way (you will probably need to do three batches). If you need to top up the oil, do. Check the chicken is cooked through before serving.

Transfer the cooked chicken to a serving platter along with the lettuce leaves, radishes, chives and honey mustard sauce, plus hot sauce, if you like. Get everyone to dig in!

Jacket Potato Spread

The perfect marriage of Sunday lunch and brunch, our friend Jo Maxwell cooked this for us and it was quite possibly the best meal we have ever had. To be fair, we are obsessed with Jacky Ps, so perhaps it's not that surprising that this ticked all our boxes.

Decadent yet simple, the only thing to serve hot is the potatoes – the rest is delicious at room temperature. So if you're aiming to eat this at 12pm, put the chicken on at 9am and the potatoes in at 10.30am to give them a good hour and a half.

Preparation time: 30 minutes
Cooking time: 3 hours
Serves: 6–8

8 baking potatoes

Carrot and courgette salad
(see page 179)

For the roast chicken
1 medium free-range chicken
½ lemon
5 garlic cloves

3 tbsp olive oil
salt and black pepper

For the warm side salad
2 aubergines
250g cherry tomatoes
olive oil, for drizzling
250g halloumi cheese

Essential toppings
200g smoked bacon rashers
butter
250g mature Cheddar cheese, grated

First thing in the morning, attend to the chicken. Preheat the oven to 180°C/gas 6 and place the chicken in an ovenproof dish. Pop the lemon and peeled whole garlic cloves inside the cavity, then drizzle olive oil over the outside. Sprinkle with salt and pepper.

Roast the bird for about 1 hour 10 minutes, depending on the size of it, basting every 15 minutes. When the juices are running clear, cover with foil and tea towels and set aside to rest.

While the chicken is cooking, trim and chop the aubergines into 3cm chunks and place in another ovenproof dish. Add the cherry tomatoes, drizzle with olive oil and sprinkle over plenty of salt and pepper. Mix, then

place in the oven with the chicken and cook until the tomatoes have burst and the aubergines are nice and golden, usually about 40 minutes. Place in a serving dish and set aside.

When the chicken and aubergines are out of the oven it's time to attend to the baked potatoes. They will need a good 1½–2 hours (depending on size) to cook to perfection. Turn the oven up to 225°C/gas 7 and place them straight in. While they are cooking, make the carrot and courgette salad and set aside.

Once the chicken is cool enough to handle, tear it into smallish pieces and place in a dish.

(continued overleaf)

About 15 minutes before your baked potatoes are ready, place a griddle pan over a medium heat. Slice the halloumi and cook on the griddle until soft and charred lines have appeared on both sides. Add to the dish of roasted aubergine and tomatoes.

Pop the bacon rashers in the griddle pan and cook until crispy in places, about 5 minutes, turning halfway to cook evenly.

Place all the accompaniments and fillings on the table alongside some butter, the grated Cheddar and some salt and pepper. Pop a baked potato on everyone's plate, then set a good example by overloading yours with too much of every topping.

'Nduja and Egg Pizza

Sometimes – often even – the best things are eaten alone, standing furtively in the privacy of the fridge door. You'll know this if you've ever had the good fortune to open your fridge in the morning and find a plate of leftover pizza nestled next to the semi-skimmed, and you'll also know that there is no finer way to start the day than with a slice or three. This recipe celebrates the notion of the 'breakfast pizza' in all its glory. It's also perfect for sharing – ideal for a sociable brunch.

Preparation time: 40 minutes, plus resting
Cooking time: 55 minutes
Serves: 6–8 (makes 2 large pizzas)

1 x 400g tin plum tomatoes
small bunch of basil (about 40g)
large pinch of sea salt
1 tbsp olive oil, plus an extra splash
2 x 250g balls of mozzarella
180g 'nduja sausage
100g rocket, washed
8 eggs
salt and black pepper

For the dough
300ml tepid water
2 tbsp olive oil
1 tsp sugar
1 x 7g sachet fast-action dried yeast
250g '00' flour
300g strong white bread flour
½ tbsp fine sea salt
fine semolina, for dusting
hot sauce (optional)

First make the pizza dough: in a bowl, mix together the water, oil, sugar and yeast.

Whisk the flours and salt together in a large bowl and make a well in the centre. Add the yeast mixture bit by bit, bringing it all together with your hands or a wooden spoon until a dough forms.

Turn onto a floured surface and knead for around 10 minutes, until supple and springy. Place in a large oiled bowl, cover with cling film and leave in a warm place for at least 1 hour.

While the dough is rising, make your sauce: add the tinned tomatoes to a small pan over a low to medium heat. Add a splash of water to the tin and give it a swirl to gather up the remaining juice, then pour it into the pan. Finely slice the leaves from a couple of sprigs of basil and add to the pan along with the salt and tablespoon of olive oil. Leave to cook for 45–60 minutes, stirring from time to time and crushing the tomatoes with the back of your spoon. The sauce should be reduced and glossy.

Preheat the oven to 250°C/gas 8 or as hot as your oven will go, and place two large baking trays inside to heat up.

Lightly flour a work surface large enough to roll out the dough. Divide the dough into two equal-sized balls. Leave to sit while you tidy and get your toppings ready.

Squeeze as much liquid out of the mozzarella as you can, then pat dry with kitchen paper: this is important or it'll make the pizzas soggy. Cut into thinish slices. Remove the skin from the 'nduja and crumble the meat. Tear the remaining basil leaves in a bowl with the rocket.

Roll out the two balls of dough to roughly the same size as the trays in the oven, trying to keep as even a thickness as possible. Take the trays from the oven, sprinkle over some semolina and place a sheet of rolled dough on each one, pushing it out with your fingers to reach the edges. Spread a thin layer of tomato sauce over the dough, then dot with chunks of 'nduja and mozzarella. Bake for 4 minutes, then remove from the oven, crack 4 eggs onto each pizza and bake for another 4–5 minutes, until the egg whites are set and the dough is golden brown and crisp.

Take the pizzas out of the oven and cut each into 16 squares. Top with the rocket and remaining basil leaves, drizzle over a splash of olive oil and season, then serve immediately.

Lentil Falafel with Baba Ghanoush

Caroline helped make thousands of these when working in the charity kitchens at the Calais camps. This is a slightly scaled-down version for about 25 of the delicious little balls, fear not. Great for a greedy brunch full of lots of different nibbly things: olives, cured meats, toasted pittas, the Jerusalem salad on page 176, and perhaps a little buttery rice, too.

You could absolutely prepare the baba ghanoush the day before it's needed and keep it in the fridge. The same goes for the falafel mixture – simply fry once your guests arrive (or just before they do). The falafels take no time at all to cook once you've got the oil hot enough.

Preparation time: 30 minutes
Cooking time: 1 hour
Serves: 4 (makes about 20–25 falafel)

For the baba ghanoush
3 aubergines
juice of ½ lemon
1½ tbsp olive oil
3 tbsp tahini
salt and black pepper

For the falafel
300g green lentils
1 tbsp extra-virgin olive oil
1 red onion, finely chopped
1½ red chillies, deseeded and
    finely chopped
small bunch of fresh coriander, stalks
    and leaves chopped separately
2 tsp ground cumin
2 tsp ground coriander
2 eggs
4 tbsp sesame seeds
450ml sunflower oil
pitta breads, to serve

First make the baba ghanoush. If you have gas rings, light 3 of them and place the aubergines directly on the flames. Cook for about 15–20 minutes, turning every so often to blister evenly. Once the aubergines are floppy, they are cooked. If you don't have a gas hob, pierce the aubergines and place them in a 180°C/gas 4 oven for 30–40 minutes until floppy.

Place the cooked aubergines in a sieve and leave until cool enough to handle. Peel off all the skin and place the flesh back in the sieve over a bowl to drain off the excess water. Roughly chop the flesh (or squeeze with

clean hands) and place in a bowl along with the remaining ingredients. Mix to combine, then taste and adjust the seasoning. Set aside or cover and place in the fridge if making the night before.

Start the falafels: place the lentils in a pan and cover with plenty of water. Bring to the boil, then simmer for 25 minutes or until cooked. Leave to cool, then tip into a food processor or blender and blitz to a smoothish consistency. Season to taste with olive oil, salt and pepper; it's important to get this right, so make sure you take the time to do this properly. Add the chopped onion, chillies and coriander stalks to the blended lentils. Follow with the remaining spices and the eggs, then mix well. This mixture can be covered and sit happily overnight in the fridge. Break off a clementine sized amout of the falafel mix and roll between your hands into a ball. Scatter the sesame seeds on your chopping board, then roll the falafel in them.

Place a 4cm depth of sunflower oil in a medium pan and heat to 180°C. Pop the falafel in, three or so at a time (you'll know the oil is hot enough if it bubbles excitedly, but not too excitedly around the falafel as it cooks), and deep-fry for a few minutes, until dark and crispy looking. Remove carefully with a slotted spoon and drain on kitchen paper, then add the next three balls of mixture. Continue until you have cooked all the falafel, then place in a warmed serving dish. Enjoy with the baba ghanoush and some warmed pittas, plus any other extras you want to add to the table.

Bagel Brunch

There will always be a special place in our hearts for East London's Brick Lane Beigel Bake, but the best bagel we've ever eaten was at Russ & Daughters, a Jewish deli on New York's Lower East Side that's been around since 1914. After queuing for ages (then missing our turn and irritating the impatient crowd behind us by changing our minds five times), we stepped out with bagels packed with cream cheese, smoked salmon, capers, red onion and juicy slices of tomato.

Partly inspired by that bagel, this is one of our favourite brunches for when we have a few people round. The idea is that you lay out all the different toppings so that everyone can help themselves: there should be enough variety to cater to most tastes and ample opportunity to mix and match.

Although we have included a recipe for bagels in this book, if you have a good bakery nearby, we urge you to make life easy and buy them. The point of this brunch is that it shouldn't be too much effort, more a case of assembling a spread of delicious things that you and your guests can keep lazily picking at.

Preparation time: 30 minutes
Serves: 8–10

12–15 slices of the best smoked salmon
    you can afford
at least 12 bagels (see pages 180–182
    if you want to make your own)
2 x 280g tubs of cream cheese
3 lemons, cut into wedges for squeezing
a fully loaded pepper grinder

For the egg salad
9 hard-boiled eggs (see page 16)
3 tbsp mayonnaise (see page 194
    if you want to make your own)
3 tbsp Greek yoghurt
small bunch of chives (around 20g),
    finely chopped
small bunch of fresh dill (around 20g),
    finely chopped
salt and black pepper

For the tuna salad
3 x 200g tins tuna in spring water, drained
3 tbsp mayonnaise (see page 194
    if you want to make your own)
3 tbsp Greek yoghurt
150g dill pickles, finely chopped
2 bunches of spring onions, dark green
    ends discarded, then finely sliced
1 tbsp black pepper
small bunch of basil, chopped
good squeeze of lemon, to taste

Highly recommended extras
the ripest fattest tomatoes you can
    find, thinly sliced
1 small red onion, very thinly sliced
good-quality capers or caper berries
pickled beetroot, thinly sliced
beetroot pickled eggs (see page 153),
    sliced

You can make the egg and tuna salads in advance: simply mix the ingredients for each salad together and season to taste. Decant into the bowls you want to serve them in and keep covered in the fridge until 30 minutes before serving.

Similarly, lay the salmon out on a platter, cover and pop in the fridge until needed.

Prepare any of the 'extras' that need slicing, then plate up, cover with cling film and leave in a cool place.

To serve it's simply a case of laying everything out, getting everyone to the table, slicing the bagels in half (toasting them for those who like a toasted bagel) and digging in.

Brisket Buns

Like the Boston Baked Beans on page 26, this is another overnight job. Pop the meat in a low oven the night before and come morning, you'll have melt-in-the-mouth brisket ready for warmed buns and a spoonful of homemade coleslaw. As you're cooking the brisket for so long it's important to consider the size of the oven dish you're putting it in:

you want the brisket to sit in a decent 4cm of stock, so adjust the liquid accordingly.

It's worth making your own mayonnaise for the slaw, but if you don't have time, mix fresh lemon juice, salt and pepper with a few tablespoons of crème fraîche and olive oil to taste.

Preparation time: 30 minutes
Cooking time: 8 hours
Serves: 8

1 tbsp sunflower oil
1.5kg beef brisket
2 red onions, quartered
500–750ml beef stock
5 garlic cloves
black pepper

For the coleslaw
300g red cabbage, finely sliced
300g white cabbage, finely sliced
1 red onion, finely sliced
3 large carrots, shaved into ribbons
    with a potato peeler
4 tbsp homemade mayonnaise (see
    page 194, or see alternative dressing
    in introduction above)

To serve
16 soft rolls
1 jar of pickled gherkins
mustard
salt and black pepper

Preheat the oven to 120°C/gas ¼.

Place a large frying pan large over a medium heat and add the sunflower oil. Season the meat with plenty of black pepper, then sear in the frying pan until brown and 'sealed' all over. Place in an ovenproof dish where it will sit relatively snugly. Make a few incisions and insert the garlic cloves, or tuck them under the strings (if there are any).

Fry the onions in the oil remaining in the frying pan to give them a bit of colour. Add to the beef dish along with the stock (see above). Cover tightly with two layers of

kitchen foil, then place in the oven for 7–8 hours overnight. In the morning, remove from the oven and, without removing the foil, cover with tea towels to keep warm.

Put all the prepared veg into a large serving bowl. Stir in the mayonnaise a tablespoon at a time, until you're happy with the consistency. We like ours coated but not drenched.

When you're ready to serve, warm the buns in the oven while you slice the brisket. Place everything on the table and enjoy.

The Continental:

A case of going to the shops and buying coffee, croissants, juice, eggs, jam, cheese, bread and ham.

The Scandinental

Shopping list: Rye bread, smoked salmon, cured meats, yoghurt, cheese, granola, eggs, chives and dill.

$\textcircled{6}$

Fresh
and
Light(er)

The Ful Egyptian

Ful medames is a spiced fava bean stew often eaten for breakfast throughout the Middle East and North Africa. Besides being inexpensive and easy to prepare, this meal ticks lots of boxes for us: the beans are warming and saucy and cry out to be mopped up, the garlic tahini sauce adds a contrasting tang, the chopped salad a refreshing element of crunch, and the boiled egg makes it brunch. Serve with the three-ingredient flatbreads (see page 187) or any other good bread.

Preparation time: 10 minutes
Cooking time: 20–25 minutes
Serves: 4

2 tbsp olive oil
½ small red onion, diced
1 garlic clove, crushed
2 x 400g tins cooked fava beans,
    rinsed and drained
1 tsp cumin seeds, ground
½ tsp cayenne pepper, plus extra
    for sprinkling
2 tomatoes, cored and chopped
juice of 1 lemon
1–2 eggs per person, depending on hunger
large handful of parsley leaves, chopped
salt
warmed flatbreads, to serve (see page
    187 if you want to make your own)

For the chopped salad
½ small red onion, sliced into thin
    half-moons
2 tbsp lemon juice
10 cherry or plum tomatoes, quartered
8 radishes, quartered
10cm piece of cucumber, cut into
    similar sized chunks to the radishes
    and tomatoes
drizzle of olive oil

For the garlic tahini sauce
1 garlic clove
2 tsp tahini
juice of ½–1 lemon

Put a frying pan over a medium heat and add the oil. When warm, add the onion, garlic and a pinch of salt (to draw out the moisture) and cook for a few minutes, until softened and starting to caramelise. Add the beans, cumin, cayenne, tomatoes, half the lemon juice and 200ml water. Cook for 10–15 minutes over a medium to low heat until the tomatoes break down, and the liquid reduces to a reddish sauce. Taste for seasoning and adjust the salt, lemon juice and cayenne accordingly.

While the beans are cooking, give the onions for the salad a head start by putting them in a small bowl and covering with a tablespoon of lemon juice. Set aside.

For the tahini sauce, pound the garlic and a large pinch of salt to a paste using a pestle and mortar, then mix in the tahini. Add the lemon juice and a splash of water and mix until thin and drizzleable.

(continued overleaf)

Put a medium pan filled with water over a high heat. When boiling, gently lower in the eggs and cook for 8 minutes. Remove from the heat immediately and run under cold water before peeling and slicing in half.

Add the remaining chopped salad ingredients to a bowl and mix together with the remaining lemon juice, a drizzle of oil and some salt.

To serve, put a large spoonful of salad on each plate, topped with a few lemony onions. Spoon on some beans, drizzle the tahini dressing over them, then top with parsley and a sprinkle of cayenne. Nestle the egg halves on the plate and serve with flatbread for mopping.

Cured Salmon, Three Ways

Smoked salmon is always a winner at brunch, but if you want to try something special and actually (beyond the shopping) incredibly easy, try curing your own salmon. The results are unbelievably good and a little goes a long way, especially when served one of the three ways we've suggested below.

You only need to buy 500g of fish to feed four generously. Below is a mix for a simple cure, but feel free to add extra ingredients and aromatics as you see fit, from crushed blackberries, juniper berries and beetroot, through to fennel and coriander seeds.

Preparation time: 5 minutes
Curing time: 36–48 hours
Serves: 4

1 tbsp Maldon sea salt
2 tbsp Maldon smoked sea salt
3 tbsp brown sugar
500g very fresh, sushi-grade skinless
    and boneless salmon

Mix the salts and sugar together in a bowl, then rub all over the salmon. Do your best to coat it evenly, then place in a large ziplock freezer bag. Pop in the fridge and place a few jarred condiments on top of the bag to weigh down on the fish. Leave for 36–48 hours, turning every 12 hours or so. The cure will draw liquid from the salmon.

Remove the cured salmon from the bag, drain away the liquid and pat dry with kitchen paper. Slice thinly and serve in one of the following ways (any leftover salmon will keep in the fridge for a further few days):

Cured salmon with boiled eggs, rice, and sesame crunchy salad
Serve the thinly sliced salmon on hot basmati rice with a soft-boiled egg, some thinly sliced carrot and spring onion with a sprinkling of sesame seeds. Simple and delicious at any time of day.

Cured salmon with beetroot and radish salad
Serve the thinly sliced salmon on some watercress leaves with water-thin slices of raw beetroot and radish (use a mandoline). In a separate bowl mix together splashes of lime juice, rice wine vinegar, sesame oil and a little sugar to taste, then sprinkle over your salad.

Cured salmon on rye bread
Serve the thinly sliced salmon on rye bread with cream cheese and lemon juice.

Bistro Salad

Sometimes you want a salad but you also want bacon and eggs and toast: what you want is the kind of salad you might get in a Parisian bistro, a salad like this.

Preparation time: 5–10 minutes
Cooking time: 20–30 minutes
Serves: 4

1 large head of frisée lettuce (around 450g) or other 'big' lettuce
400g ripe cherry or baby plum tomatoes
1 tbsp olive oil, plus extra for drizzling
90g pancetta slices
4 eggs

4 large slices of sourdough or other bread
1 garlic clove
salt and black pepper

For the mustard dressing
1 fat garlic clove
2½ tbsp olive oil
2 tsp Dijon mustard
2 tsp wholegrain mustard
3 tbsp white wine vinegar

Wash the frisée thoroughly, then spin until as dry as possible – if you don't have a salad spinner, give it a good long shake in a colander. Line a large bowl with kitchen paper, add the frisée, then cover and leave in the fridge until needed.

Preheat the oven to 200°C/gas 6. Add the tomatoes to a foil-lined baking tray, drizzle with oil and sprinkle with salt, then roast for 15–20 minutes, or until blistered and juicy but still intact.

While the tomatoes are roasting, add the tablespoon of oil to a frying pan and put over a medium to high heat. Add the pancetta and fry until golden and crisp. Remove from the pan with a slotted spoon and leave to sit on a plate lined with kitchen paper.

To make the dressing, mash the garlic with a little salt using a pestle and mortar until paste-like, then whisk in the oil, mustards and vinegar, any juices from the roasted tomatoes, and a little of the cooled pancetta cooking oil. Taste and adjust the seasoning, then pour the dressing into the bowl you are going to serve your salad in.

Put a small pan of water on to boil. When it's bubbling away, add the eggs and cook for 7 minutes, then drain and leave to sit in cold water for a couple of minutes. Peel and cut into quarters.

Toast the bread slices. Cut the garlic clove in half and rub gently over the toast then drizzle over some olive oil.

Roughly tear up the frisée and add to the bowl with the dressing. Crumble over the pancetta and mix well.

Add a slice of toast to each plate, then top with a generous heap of salad. Sit the quartered eggs and roasted tomatoes on it and season.

Caesar Salad

A tangle of delicate leaves is all well and good, but sometimes you want something crunchy and fresh that also whacks you round the face with flavour – in a good way. At times like these, you need the umami bomb that is the Caesar salad.

You can wash the lettuce (we like to use little gem rather than the traditional romaine) and make the dressing a good few hours in advance; just keep them both in the fridge. It might seem weird to wash the lettuce ahead of time, but it keeps very well in a bowl or plastic freezer bag with a few small pieces of kitchen paper to absorb any excess water.

For a wintry Caesar, rub the dressing into roughly chopped kale or cavolo nero leaves and leave to marinate for a couple of hours (this is a good packed lunch option, as the leaves are so sturdy that they actually benefit from being pre-dressed, unlike lettuce which will go limp and soggy). Or mix things up by using bitter leaves like radicchio. If you don't feel comfortable using raw egg yolks in the dressing, you could substitute a tablespoon of ready-made mayo.

Preparation time: 10 minutes
Cooking time: 5 minutes
Serves: 4

6 little gem lettuces
4 slices of slightly stale bread
4 tbsp olive oil, for frying
Parmesan cheese, to serve

For the dressing (makes around 150ml)
2–3 garlic cloves
5 anchovies
2 tsp Dijon mustard
2 egg yolks
juice of 1 lemon (about 3 tbsp)
2 tbsp olive oil
30g Parmesan cheese, finely grated
1 tsp black pepper
sea salt

First make the dressing: mash the garlic with a little sea salt in a pestle and mortar until paste-like. Add the anchovies and mash again until they have broken down, then add the rest of the ingredients and mix together until fully combined. Taste and adjust the seasoning, adding more lemon juice or oil as necessary. Cover and chill in the fridge.

Wash and dry the lettuce leaves.

Rip the bread into rough chunks – not too big, you want them to be bite-sized. Heat the olive oil in a frying pan and fry the bread chunks over a medium heat until golden brown and crisp (around 4–5 minutes). Remove to a tray lined with kitchen paper to drain.

When you're ready to eat, add the dressing to the bowl you are going to serve the salad in. Throw in the leaves and half of the croutons and mix together with your hands. Sprinkle over the remaining croutons and shave over some Parmesan.

Roasted Citrus and Avocado Salad

Griddling the little gem lettuce gives it a lovely nutty texture that works very well alongside boiled eggs and the cured salmon on page 131.

Preparation time: 10 minutes
Cooking time: 30 minutes
Serves: 4

1 red grapefruit
drizzle of olive oil
4 little gem lettuces
1 head of chicory, leaves separated
few radicchio leaves
2 avocados

For the dressing
2 tbsp olive oil
zest and juice of ½ lemon
salt and black pepper

Preheat the oven to 180°C/gas 4. Slice the grapefruit into rounds, leaving the skin on, and place in a single layer in a couple of ovenproof dishes. Drizzle over a little olive oil, then bake for 30 minutes.

Meanwhile, place a griddle pan over a high heat. Quarter the little gem lettuces, then griddle, cut side down, until you have char marks. Set aside.

Combine the dressing ingredients in the bottom of a large salad bowl and top with the chicory, radicchio and charred little gems. Halve the avocados, slice then scoop out the flesh and add to the salad.

Remove the grapefruit from the oven once blackened in bits, then roughly chop, and add to the salad. Toss and serve immediately with plenty of bread.

Chickpeas with Greens

We often eat a variation of this for a working brunch – by which we mean an early weekday lunch that is somehow the first meal of the day, rather than a boozy Donald Draper number – as it's quick, requires one fork-holding hand to eat and takes nicely to the addition of a fried egg on top. We love using cime di rapa or chard, but you could also use kale, cavolo nero or even beetroot leaves and stalks or tenderstem broccoli – just adjust the cooking times according to toughness.

Preparation time: 5–10 minutes
Cooking time: 10–15 minutes
Serves: 2–4

1 bunch of cime di rapa or chard
(around 300g)
2 x 400g tins chickpeas,
rinsed and drained
3cm piece of fresh turmeric
(or use ¼ tsp ground turmeric)
3 tbsp rapeseed or olive oil
3 garlic cloves, thinly sliced
zest of 1 unwaxed lemon
juice of ½ unwaxed lemon,
plus extra to taste
salt and black pepper

Wash the cime di rapa or other greens and trim the stalks – get rid of anything tough, stringy or with a hollow centre. Cut off the remaining stalks and chop into roughly ½cm chunks, then roughly chop the leaves, keeping the leaves and stalks separate.

Dry the chickpeas on some kitchen paper. Peel and grate the turmeric very finely – this stuff is worse than beetroot for staining, so protect your clothes, surfaces and hands if you don't want them to take on a nicotine hue.

Add the oil to a large sauté pan over a medium heat. When hot, add the garlic and fry for 30 seconds to soften slightly before throwing in the stalks from the cime di rapa or other greens. Cook for 3–5 minutes, or until just tender.

Pour in the chickpeas, scrape in the turmeric and lemon zest and mix together with a wooden spoon until everything is coated. Fry for a couple of minutes, then add the cime di rapa leaves (or other greens) and lemon juice and pop on the lid. Cook for around 5 minutes, shuffling occasionally, until the leaves have just wilted down. Season (be generous, it needs the salt) and add an extra squeeze of lemon if you fancy.

Sausage Bun Cha

The divide between what we would like to eat and what we think we should eat often feels most pronounced at breakfast or brunch time, when the appeal of a fruit salad can wane next to a fry-up. There's a time for both, of course, but for moments when you want salty and fatty *and* crisp and fresh, there is Vietnamese bun cha.

Preparation time: 10 minutes
Cooking time: 20 minutes
Serves: 4

2 soft lettuces
large bunch of Thai (or regular) basil
large bunch of perilla (or mint)
large bunch of hot mint (or coriander)
2 watermelon radishes or 12 normal
  radishes, halved
6 spring onions, thinly sliced
3 tbsp rice or cider vinegar
pinch of salt
pinch of palm sugar (or brown sugar)
500g vermicelli rice noodles

For the dressing
8 garlic cloves
4 tbsp palm sugar (or brown sugar)
4 bird's-eye chillies, deseeded and very
  finely chopped or sliced
60ml fish sauce
180ml rice or cider vinegar

For the sausage patties
6 garlic cloves
2 tbsp palm sugar (or brown sugar)
2 tbsp fish sauce
12 pork sausages
vegetable oil, for frying

Wash and dry the lettuce and herbs (you can do this in advance, see page 133).

Add the radishes and spring onions to a bowl with the vinegar, salt and sugar and scrunch together with your hands, then set aside.

To make the dressing, crush the garlic and sugar to a paste using a pestle and mortar. Add the chilli and bash lightly to release some of its juices then mix in the fish sauce and vinegar. Taste and adjust seasoning if necessary: it should be sweet and salty and sour and spicy.

Cook the noodles in boiling water, according to the packet instructions, then drain and leave to cool.

To make the sausage patties, mash the garlic and sugar to a paste using a pestle and mortar, then add the fish sauce. Slit the sausages and squeeze the meat into a large bowl. Mix in the garlic paste, then form the mixture into 16 patties.

Grease a griddle pan with a little oil and put over a medium heat. When hot cook the patties in batches for about 5 minutes on each side until really browned and crisp.

When you're ready to eat, shred the lettuce. Divide the noodles between four large bowls, then top with the lettuce, some herbs, radish and sausage patties. Serve with the dressing for drizzling and extra herbs.

Fruit Salads

It's always lovely to add a bit of colour and fibre to an otherwise beige table of bread, eggs and hash browns. Finish your fruit medleys with flavoursome extras as you see fit, such as a sprinkling of icing sugar, a pinch of cinnamon, a handful of fresh mint leaves or some ground cardamom.

Each salad below serves 6–8

Rhubarb compote with fresh strawberries
Our friend, the inimitable Juliet Annan, made this for dessert once after a simple supper of homemade Scotch eggs and asparagus. Make the rhubarb compote on page 132, omitting the ginger, and leave to cool to room temperature. When you're about to serve, stir in 250g sliced strawberries. Spoon on top of yoghurt and granola, or enjoy alongside a slice of the coffee and banana loaf on page 161.

Winter sun
Using a large sharp knife, chop the leafy crown off one small pineapple. Place it cut end down and slice the tough skin off in a downward motion, following the contours of the fruit. Slice and chop the peeled flesh into generous pieces and place in a serving bowl. Add 2 oranges and 4 kiwis, peeled and cut into chunks, followed by the seeds of half a pomegranate. Combine and keep in the fridge until you are ready to serve.

Spring
Combine 250g washed and sliced strawberries in a serving bowl. Add 150g washed blueberries and about half a small watermelon, first sliced into wedges, then flesh scooped off the rind and chopped into chunks (or use a melon baller if you have one gathering dust in a drawer somewhere). Keep in the fridge until you are ready to serve.

Summer
Slice 2 large mangoes laterally either side of the stones, as close as you can to them, then make criss-cross incisions in the flesh, without piercing the skin. Push the flesh outwards using your fingers, slice off the chunks and place in a serving bowl. Salvage any further flesh from around the stones and add to the dish. Next, chop a cantaloupe melon in half, then slice into wedges. Remove the seeds, then slice the flesh off the rind with a sharp knife. Chop roughly and add to the mango, along with 250g washed and halved grapes. This mixture will keep in the fridge for a few hours until you are ready to serve.

⑦

Savouries

Devilled Eggs

Unapologetically 1970s but completely
delicious – a brunch canapé of sorts.

Preparation time: 5 minutes
Cooking time: 8 minutes
Serves: 6 (2 halves each)

6 eggs
½ ripe avocado

squeeze of lime juice
50g cooked prawns, roughly chopped
2 tbsp mayonnaise (ideally homemade,
    see page 194)
6 sprigs of coriander (or 1 tbsp
    snipped cress)
salt

Place a pan of water on to boil and, once
bubbling, gently add the eggs. Boil for 8
minutes then drain and run under the cold
tap to cool.

Scoop the avocado flesh into a bowl, mash,
then sprinkle over some salt and a little
squeeze of lime juice. Add the chopped
prawns followed by the mayonnaise and
mix well.

Carefully peel the cooled eggs and slice
in half. Remove the yolks and add to the
avocado mix. Stir to combine, then put
heaped tablespoons into the egg hollows.
Arrange on a plate and finish with some
coriander leaves. Chill until you are ready
to serve.

Oeufs Mimosa

Caroline used to gorge on this retro classic on Christmas Eve in Provence. It makes a nice gluten-free addition to any brunch.

Preparation time: 5 minutes
Cooking time: 8 minutes
Serves: 6 (2 halves each)

6 eggs
1 x 160g tin tuna chunks, drained
2 tbsp mayonnaise (ideally homemade, see page 194)

1 tsp capers, finely chopped
1 tbsp fresh parsley, finely chopped
½ tsp smoked paprika, plus extra for sprinkling
black pepper

Place a pan of water on to boil and, once bubbling, gently add the eggs. Boil for 8 minutes then drain and run under the cold tap to cool.

Tip the tuna into a bowl and add the mayonnaise, capers, parsley, paprika and pepper to taste. Mix well.

Carefully peel the cooled eggs and slice in half. Remove the yolks and add to the tuna mix. Stir well to combine, then put heaped tablespoons into the egg hollows.

Arrange on a plate and finish with a final sprinkling of paprika. Chill until you are ready to serve.

Welsh Rabbit

Fancy cheese on toast for the
discerning bruncher.

Preparation time: 3 minutes
Cooking time: 5 minutes
Serves: 6 (as a nibble), or 3 as a
   more substantial brunch course

10g butter, plus extra for spreading
10g plain flour

100ml stout
50ml milk
100g Cheddar cheese, grated
3 slices of bread
splash of Worcestershire sauce
black pepper

Melt the butter in a small pan over a
medium heat and add the flour. Stir with a
wooden spoon to combine and cook a little
then pour in the stout, followed by the milk.

Continue stirring until smooth and hot,
then mix in the grated Cheddar.

Preheat the grill to high and lightly toast the
bread. Butter it on both sides, then pour
over your cheese mixture. Add a dash of
Worcestershire sauce on each followed by
some black pepper, then finish under the
grill until the cheese is almost molten. Cut
each slice in quarters and serve immediately.

Devils on Horseback

Keep a tray of these in the fridge, ready
to bang in the oven and bake when your
guests arrive.

Preparation time: 5 minutes
Cooking time: 10 minutes
Serves: 6–8 (makes about 30)

250g smoked streaky bacon rashers
300g pitted soft prunes

Preheat the grill to 180°C/gas 4 and line a
large baking tray with foil.

Chop each rasher of bacon into two or
three segments (depending on the length
of the rashers). Wrap each slice of bacon
around a single prune and secure with a
cocktail stick.

Continue until you have used up all the
bacon or prunes, and place on the lined
baking tray.

Cook in the oven for 10 minutes, or until the
bacon is nice and crispy (you might need to
flip them to cook evenly). Serve immediately.

Smoked Kippers with Bread and Butter

A delicious and surprisingly filling wintry brunch, a big mug of builder's tea feels obligatory alongside this. Kippers usually come butterflied, i.e. sliced in half and 'flattened', which makes them very quick to cook.

Cooking time: 5 minutes
Serves: 2

knob of unsalted butter, plus extra
    for the toast
2 smoked kippers
2 slices of bread

Place a frying pan over a medium heat and add the knob of butter. Once melted, add the smoked kippers and fry for 2 minutes on each side to heat through.

While the fish is cooking, toast the bread and then butter generously. Serve with the kippers and eat immediately, avoiding the fish bones.

Scotch Woodcock

Like Welsh Rabbit, no animals are actually used in this dish. Allow for half a slice of toast per person as part of a traditional savoury course for six (e.g. alongside the Devils on Horseback and the Kippers, pages 149 and opposite), or for three as a more substantial brunch course.

Preparation time: 2 minutes
Cooking time: 10 minutes
Serves: 6

6 eggs
splash of milk

generous knob of butter, plus extra
  for spreading
4 anchovies
1 tbsp finely grated Parmesan cheese
3 slices of bread
salt and black pepper

Crack the eggs into a bowl and add the milk and some pepper. Whisk until combined.

Melt the butter in a frying pan over a low heat and add the anchovies. Cook for a minute or two, stirring with a wooden spoon, until they have dissolved.

Add the egg mixture and stir with a wooden spoon until cooked. The key is to do this slowly, so don't be tempted to crank the heat up.

Sprinkle over the Parmesan when the eggs are starting to look cooked and keep stirring until you achieve a scrambled egg consistency. Taste to check the seasoning, adjusting with salt if needed (you might not need any as the anchovies are salty).

Toast the bread, butter it, then slice each piece in half diagonally. Spread the eggs on each slice and finish with a final sprinkling of pepper.

Beetroot Pickled Eggs

Pickling eggs – even very lightly – gives them a lovely firm texture, while the beetroot turns them a pretty wild colour. These are great paired with anything rich or fatty: smoked or cured salmon (see page 131), latkes (see page 191), or labneh (see page 193) or cream cheese on toast. Or you could recreate a classic pub snack and add them to a bag of crushed crisps... The pickled beets you are left with at the end are good in a salad or on a bagel.

Preparation time: 2 minutes, plus chilling
Cooking time: 10 minutes
Makes: 6 eggs (to fit in 1 large jar)

350ml cider vinegar
150ml water

¼ tsp salt
1 tsp sugar
½ tsp black peppercorns
½ tsp fennel seeds
1 small beetroot, peeled and thinly sliced
6 eggs

Add the vinegar, water, salt, sugar and spices to a pan and bring to the boil, then remove from the heat. Add the sliced beetroot and leave to cool.

Put a pan of water on to boil. Once bubbling, carefully add the eggs and cook for 8½ minutes at a steady simmer. Drain immediately and cover with cold water; leave to sit for a couple of minutes, then peel.

Add the eggs to a scrupulously clean jar or container, then carefully pour in the beetroot and pickling liquid (this shouldn't be stone cold but cool enough not to crack your jar). Chill in the fridge for at least 2 hours before serving. The egg will be good for a couple of weeks and will increase in intensity the longer you leave them (we prefer them slightly milder).

Veggie Scotch Eggs

With an egg in the middle and a breakfast cereal coating, these are surely the ultimate brunch treat.

Preparation time: 30 minutes
Cooking time: 15 minutes
Serves: 5

25g butter
1 onion, finely chopped
2 garlic cloves, finely chopped
small bunch of parsley, chopped
1 tsp chilli flakes
pinch of dried thyme
splash of white wine

2 x 400g tins butterbeans or
  cannellini beans, rinsed and drained
1 tbsp plain or gram (chickpea) flour,
  plus extra for rolling
5 hard-boiled eggs, peeled
1 egg, beaten
200g Rice Krispies, slightly crushed
  by hand
1 litre vegetable oil
salt and black pepper

Melt the butter in a frying pan and add the onion, garlic, parsley, chilli flakes and thyme. Sweat over a low heat for 15 minutes, adding some more butter if it starts to look too dry. Turn the heat up, add the white wine and allow the liquid to evaporate completely. Remove from the heat and leave to cool.

Meanwhile, blend the beans using a stick blender and mix in a tablespoon or so of the flour. Season with plenty of salt and pepper, then add the cooled onion mix.

Prepare a workstation with your peeled boiled eggs, your bean mix and bowls of flour, beaten egg and Rice Krispies.

Squeeze a handful of the bean mix around an egg, ensuring there are no air holes or gaps. Dunk in the flour bowl to coat (shake off any excess) followed by the beaten egg and the Rice Krispies. Tightly press the Krispies around the mix, making you have covered the whole surface.

Put the vegetable oil in a large flameproof casserole dish, making sure the oil comes only halfway up the sides. Heat slowly to 180°C – test the temperature by dropping in a few Rice Krispies; they should sizzle gently.

Now, using a slotted spoon, gently lower up to 3 scotch eggs into the oil one at a time and cook for 4 minutes, or until golden. Remove with a slotted spoon and drain on kitchen paper. Cook the remaining eggs in the same way.

8

That Sweet Spot

Granola

This is our favourite granola mix. It's worth looking out for special offers in pound shops and the like for the ingredients, as they can add up a bit if you go to a supermarket, which somehow defeats the object of making granola oneself. We like set honey as it tends to be of a better quality; if you prefer the runny version, try to get one that isn't from a blend of honeys – aim for one that comes from one happy location.

Double the quantities here if you want to make enough for one of those pleasing big Kilner jars.

Preparation time: 5 minutes
Cooking time: 40 minutes
Makes: 8–10 servings

1 heaped tbsp coconut oil
100ml honey
150g chunky rolled oats

25g flaked almonds
50g pecans, chopped
10g pumpkin seeds
10g sunflower seeds
20g coconut flakes
10g dried cranberries
10g dried apricots

Preheat the oven to 140°C/gas 1 and line a baking tray with baking paper.

Place the coconut oil and honey in a small pan and heat very gently for a few minutes to melt and combine.

Place the oats and all the nuts, seeds and flakes in a large bowl and mix well. Pour in the melted honey and oil and mix well to combine.

Spread the granola mix over the baking tray as thinly as possible and place in the oven for about 40 minutes or until golden, stirring every 5–10 minutes or so to cook evenly. Don't worry too much about the oats seeming soft; as long as they become golden, they will crisp up as they cool. Once cool, place the granola in an airtight container and mix in the dried fruit.

Enjoy this on its own with milk or sprinkled over yoghurt and a fruit compote (see pages 167–168).

Porridge with Rum-caramelised Banana

A fiery spectacle of a brunch, this is one for a special occasion.

Preparation time: 10 minutes
Cooking time: 30 minutes
Serves: 4

50g hazelnuts
3 bananas

40g butter
30g soft brown sugar
200g jumbo porridge oats
600ml water
100ml milk, plus extra
2 tbsp dark rum

Dry-roast the whole hazelnuts for a few minutes in a frying pan until the skins blacken and start falling off. Set aside to cool, then chop roughly.

Peel and halve 2 of the bananas down the middle lengthways. If they are large, cut them also through the middle widthways so that you end up with 8 pieces.

Wipe the hazelnut pan clean and melt the butter and brown sugar over a medium heat. Arrange the banana pieces snugly in the pan and leave to cook over a medium heat for 3–4 minutes on each side.

Meanwhile, make the porridge using the method on page 38. Roughly chop the remaining banana and stir through the porridge as it simmers. Add the milk and stir vigorously. Pour into four bowls and prepare the banana flambé.

Have a lighter or box of matches ready. Make sure your cooker hood is turned off. Turn up the heat under the bananas for a minute. Take the pan off the heat, quickly pour the rum over the bananas, then return to the heat and set fire to the rum. Leave to bubble for a couple of minutes after the flames have died down.

Lay the flambéed banana pieces carefully over the porridge and pour over the buttery rummy juices. Sprinkle the chopped hazelnuts over the top and enjoy.

Coffee and Banana Loaf

Serve with fresh coffee, seasonal fruit and
dollops of mascarpone.

Preparation time: 15 minutes
Cooking time: 45 minutes
Serves: 8

50ml strong black coffee
110g butter, plus extra for greasing
225g caster sugar

2 ripe bananas
2 eggs
100g ground almonds
50g walnuts, roughly chopped
225g plain flour
1 tbsp baking powder

Preheat the oven to 180°C/gas 4. Grease
and line a 900g loaf tin with baking paper.

Prepare the coffee (essentially you're making
a double espresso here) and set aside to cool.

In a large bowl, cream the butter and sugar
together until light and fluffy – use a hand-
held electric mixer if you have one. Mash the
bananas, then add to the mixture along with
the eggs. Beat until combined, then add the
cooled coffee, ground almonds and walnuts.

Sift the flour and baking powder onto the
mixture, then carefully fold in. As soon as
there is no more visible flour, stop folding
and spoon the batter into your prepared tin.

Bake for 45 minutes on the middle shelf of
your oven. Check it's cooked by skewering
the middle with a knife and ensuring the
blade comes out clean. Turn onto a wire
rack and leave to cool before peeling off the
paper and serving.

Blueberry and Rhubarb Muffins

The addition of summer rhubarb makes this classic muffin extra fruity and beautifully splodged through with pink and purple.

If rhubarb's not in season, you could use a couple of grated apples instead or just keep it simple with the blueberries.

Preparation time: 20 minutes
Cooking time: 20–30 minutes
Makes: 12 muffins

150g rhubarb (around 3 stalks)
300g plain flour
2 tsp baking powder
1 tsp bicarbonate of soda
½ tsp salt
zest of 1 unwaxed lemon

200g caster sugar
75g unsalted butter, slightly softened
   and roughly chopped
2 eggs
220g Greek yoghurt
300g blueberries
muffin cases/greaseproof paper
2 tbsp pistachios, roughly chopped
   (optional)

Preheat the oven to 180°C/gas 4 and line a 12-hole muffin tin with paper or muffin cases.

Slice the rhubarb stalks in quarters lengthways. Chop these thin sticks into ½cm pieces.

In a medium bowl, whisk together the flour, baking powder, bicarbonate of soda, and salt.

In a large bowl, rub the lemon zest into the sugar. Mix in the butter with a wooden spoon until combined. Beat in the eggs one by one, then mix in the yoghurt. Fold in the flour mix here, followed by the chopped rhubarb and 250g of the blueberries. Don't overmix but make sure the fruit is evenly distributed.

Spoon the mixture equally into the muffin cases. Top with the remaining blueberries and a sprinkle of pistachios.

Bake for 20–30 minutes, until a skewer or sharp knife poked in the middle of a muffin comes out clean (we normally set our timer for 20 minutes, then rotate the tray so the muffins brown evenly). Leave to cool on a wire rack before eating.

Sour Cherry Compote

A little goes a long way with this intense sour-sweet compote. We like it with peanut butter on toast but it goes surprisingly well with a cheese toastie too (see page 83). It is pretty jammy, so any leftovers will keep in an airtight container for up to a month.

Preparation time: 2 minutes
Cooking time: 20–25 minutes
Makes: about 250g

500g frozen cherries, thawed
zest and juice of ½ lemon
2 tbsp pomegranate molasses
2 tbsp caster sugar

Add all the ingredients to a heavy-based pan and place over a low to medium heat. Cook gently for 15 minutes until the sugar has dissolved.

Increase the heat to high and cook for another 5–10 minutes or so, stirring occasionally (and lowering the heat, if necessary) to stop it burning, until the mixture is sticky enough to coat the back of the spoon. Leave to cool before eating or chill in the fridge until needed.

Spiced Rhubarb Compote

Our friend Tamsin made a variation on this rhubarb for us, serving it in small glasses with yoghurt and a spoonful of granola – a perfect little starter for a special brunch.

Preparation time: 5 minutes
Cooking time: 15 minutes
Makes: about 600g

600g rhubarb
zest and juice of ½ lemon

3cm piece of fresh ginger, peeled and
  finely grated (a microplane is handy here)
1 star anise
10 tbsp caster sugar

Cut any very fat rhubarb stalks in half lengthways, then chop them all on the diagonal into 3cm chunks.

Add the fruit to a heavy-based pan with the rest of the ingredients and cook over a low to medium heat for around 10–15 minutes, until the rhubarb is just tender. Remove from the heat and leave to cool before eating, or chill in the fridge until needed.

Cinnamon Buns with Cream Cheese Icing

Somewhere between a sticky bun and an American iced cinnamon roll, these pastries are just as good with builder's tea as they are with filter coffee.

Baking with yeast requires time: on the plus side, it's not as though you have to be anxiously hovering around the kitchen. Say you start these at 6pm: by 6.30pm you should be able to leave the dough for its first prove, leaving you free to make dinner, watch TV or mindlessly browse the internet (whatever floats your boat). By 9pm the dough will be ready to knock back and roll, then you can chill the shaped buns overnight (the cold temperature slows down the yeast, preventing them from over-proving). When you wake up, they'll be ready to bake.

Bar bacon frying or coffee brewing, there are few things more pleasant or enticing than the smell of cinnamon buns baking, and any annoyance you might have felt at the mild faff of the thing will soon be forgotten as you take your first bite of a just-iced bun.

For a Chelsea-style bun, add 250g currants to the filling.

Preparation time: 1 hour, plus proving and chilling
Cooking time: 30 minutes
Makes: 12 large buns

350ml milk
75g unsalted butter, plus extra for greasing
2 x 7g sachets fast-action dried yeast
750g plain flour, plus extra for dusting
75g sugar
½ tsp salt
100g yoghurt or buttermilk
oil for greasing

50g demerara sugar
milk, for brushing

For the filling
50g unsalted butter
200g soft brown sugar
2 tbsp ground cinnamon
½ tbsp allspice

For the icing
120g cream cheese
40g icing sugar
pinch of salt (optional)

In a small pan, warm the milk over a medium heat (don't let it bubble), then add the butter and leave to melt. Sprinkle over the yeast and mix together until any lumps dissolve.

Whisk the flour, sugar and salt together in a large bowl. Gradually add the milk-butter mixture, mixing together with a wooden spoon. When combined, add the yoghurt or buttermilk and mix again.

The dough should be fairly sticky, with an almost porridge-like consistency.

Flour your work surface generously, turn the dough onto it and knead until smooth and supple – this should take about 5–10 minutes. Grease a large bowl with a little oil, add the dough to it and cover with cling film. Leave somewhere warm for 2 hours.

While the dough is proving you can make the filling. Melt the butter and leave to cool slightly. Combine the sugar and spices in a small bowl.

When the dough has doubled in size, line a large rectangular baking tray with greaseproof paper, grease with a little butter and sprinkle with the demerara sugar. Clear a large area of your work surface and lightly flour. Turn out the dough, punch it down and roll out to a large, even rectangle – around ½cm thick and 50 x 35cm. Brush the butter over the dough, then sprinkle over the sugar and spices, covering it right up to the edges.

Roll the longer side of the dough in on itself to make a fat sausage – try to keep it as even as you can so you end up with similar sized buns. Cut the dough sausage in half, then cut the two halves in half again so you have 4 pieces. Cut each of these into 3 equal pieces. Place on your lined tray, spacing them a couple of centimetres apart, then cover with cling film and leave for at least an hour, or pop in the fridge overnight.

In the morning, or when you're ready to bake, preheat the oven to 180°C/gas 4. Remove the buns from the fridge (if necessary) and brush the tops with milk – this will help them to turn a nice golden brown. Bake in the hot oven for 30 minutes.

Beat the icing ingredients together in a bowl and spread on the buns a couple of minutes after removing from the oven. Eat immediately.

9

Extras

Jerusalem Salad

This delicious salad recipe, donated by Caroline's youngest sister Estelle, goes with just about everything, providing colour, texture and freshness to even the naughtiest brunch. Enjoy with the Mediterranean salad on page 58 or the falafel on page 114-115.

Preparation time: 5 mins
Serves: 6

500g tomatoes, finely chopped
350g cucumber (about 25cm),
   finely chopped
1 red onion, finely chopped
small bunch of fresh dill, finely chopped
juice of ½ lemon
1 tbsp extra-virgin olive oil
salt and black pepper

Place the tomatoes, cucumber, red onion and dill in a large bowl. Mix together, then add the lemon juice and season to taste. Finish with a drizzle of olive oil.

Carrot and Courgette Salad

We probably make a variation on this salad most weeks for our work packed lunches. We don't like it too oily so the lemon juice here is very important.

Preparation time: 5 minutes
Serves: 6, as part of a meal

2 small courgettes
3 large carrots
1 garlic clove, crushed

juice of 1 lemon
1 tbsp olive oil
2 tsp sesame oil
2 tbsp mixed seeds e.g. pumpkin
  and sunflower
salt and black pepper

Trim the carrots and courgettes, then shave into ribbons (using a potato peeler) and place in a bowl.

When you are ready to serve, add the garlic and lemon juice to the carrot, followed by the oils and salt and pepper. Mix well, then sprinkle over the seeds and serve.

Bagels

This method is indebted to Peter Reinhart's definitive bagel recipe. We love supporting our local bakeries and, if you want to make life simple, you can buy great bagels. On the other hand, if you've always had a yen to learn how to make them yourself, why not give it a go. It's time consuming, yes, but not as difficult as you might think, and you can adapt the master recipe below to make harder-to-find flavours like cinnamon sultana rye (see page 182 and pictured opposite with our favourite topping of peanut butter).

Preparation time: 40 minutes, plus proving and chilling
Cooking time: 45 minutes
Makes: 12

425ml tepid water
2 tbsp honey
1 x 7g sachet fast-action dried yeast

800g very strong white bread flour, plus extra for dusting
vegetable or sunflower oil spray
semolina, for sprinkling
1 large egg white
4 tbsp mixed seeds (sesame, poppy, whatever you like)
salt

Add the water, honey and yeast to a bowl and mix together until the yeast has dissolved. Leave for 15 minutes: this is not essential but it's a way to check your yeast is good – if it is, it should go frothy.

In a large bowl, whisk together the flour and a good pinch of salt, then mix in the yeast mixture until combined. Turn onto a clean surface (you shouldn't need flour) and knead for 5–10 minutes until the dough comes together and is smooth and supple. It might seem a bit dry at first but it will get there eventually.

Place the dough in a large, lightly greased bowl, cover with cling film, and leave to rise somewhere warm for an hour.

Punch down the dough. Divide into 12 equal portions – the best way to do this is to weigh the dough and then divide by 12 to calculate how much each bagel should weigh (they should be around 100–120g each). Roll each portion into a ball and then poke a finger through the middle to make a hole and mould into a bagel shape. Alternatively, roll each portion into a sausage about 20cm long and wrap around your fingers so the two ends sit on the inside of your hand. Line them up so they overlap by around 5cm and squidge together by closing your hand into a fist. Make sure the seal is smooth and the bagel is even.

Line a couple of baking trays with greaseproof paper and spray with oil. Place the bagels on the tray, spray with more oil (to stop them sticking), then cover with cling film and chill in the fridge overnight.

In the morning, take the bagels from the fridge. Preheat the oven to 200°C/gas 6 and place a couple of baking sheets inside to heat. Put a large pan of water on to boil.

(continued overleaf)

When the water is boiling, carefully add 2 bagels at a time (don't overcrowd the pan). A metal slotted spoon or spatula is useful here. Boil for a minute, then flip over and boil for another minute. Transfer to a wire rack. Repeat this step until all the bagels are cooked.

Take the heated baking trays from the oven, line with baking paper and sprinkle with semolina. Place the boiled bagels on the trays, brush with the egg white and sprinkle over the seeds. Bake for 20 minutes until golden brown.

Allow to cool slightly before serving. Any spare bagels can be wrapped and saved for up to 3 days, or sliced in half, wrapped and frozen for easy toasting.

Onion bagels

Caramelise 2 very thinly sliced onions in a tablespoon of oil with good pinch of salt over a low heat for 40 minutes. Leave to cool. Add to the supple kneaded dough, then continue kneading until the onions are evenly distributed in it. Shape, boil and bake as described on page 180, adding ½ tablespoon of caraway seeds to the seed mix they're finished with.

Cinnamon sultana rye bagels

Use 450ml tepid water, 500g very strong white bread flour and 300g rye flour in the basic dough and knead until supple. Mix together 3 tablespoons of ground cinnamon, 2 tablespoons of brown sugar and 250g sultanas and knead into the dough until evenly distributed. Shape, boil and bake as described on page 180.

Mackerel Pâté with Pickles

Serve with spelt crispbreads (see page 186),
a pile of attractive salad leaves and some
warm boiled eggs.

Preparation time: 20 minutes, plus resting
Cooking time: 8 minutes
Serves: 4

10g butter
4 shallots, thinly sliced
250g smoked mackerel fillets
3 heaped tbsp crème fraîche
1 tsp curry powder
squeeze of lemon juice (optional)

For the quick pickled cucumber
10cm cucumber, peeled into ribbons
60ml white wine vinegar
1 tbsp sea salt flakes
1 tbsp sugar
few sprigs of dill, to garnish

For the quick pickled cabbage
50g red cabbage, finely shredded
60ml white wine vinegar
1 tbsp sea salt flakes
1 tbsp sugar
few sprigs of dill, to garnish

Melt the butter in a frying pan over a medium heat. Add the shallots to the pan and cook for 8–10 minutes until they start to take on some colour and crisp a little. Set aside to cool.

Meanwhile, using a fork, scrape the mackerel flesh away from its skin and place in a bowl (discarding the skin and any bones). Mash the fish with the fork and add the remaining ingredients. Taste to check the seasoning (add a squeeze of lemon juice if you wish). Stir in the crispy shallots, then pop the bowl in the fridge until you are ready to serve.

To make the pickled vegetables, simply combine the ingredients in bowls and leave to rest for 10 minutes. Drain, rinsing off any excess pickling liquid, and replace in the bowls. Finish with a few sprigs of dill.

English Muffins

Make the dough in advance and leave to prove overnight in the fridge. Traditionally, muffins are cooked on the hob, which is how they get their telltale brown circles.

Don't be tempted to increase the heat to speed up the cooking time: you'll get a raw doughy middle and a burnt bottom.

Preparation time: 30 minutes, plus proving
Cooking time: 40 minutes
Makes: 6

250ml milk
1 x 7g sachet fast-action dried yeast

1 tbsp sugar
300g plain flour
1 tsp salt
20g chilled unsalted butter, diced plus
    extra for frying
oil, for greasing

Place the milk in a pan and heat until warm. Add the yeast and sugar, whisk together, then leave for an hour until the top is nice and frothy.

Sift the flour and salt into a bowl and form a well in the centre. Add the diced butter, then the frothy milk and gradually mix to form a wet dough. Place the dough on a work surface and knead. Don't worry if it feels wet: it starts this way but will come together. Knead for about 15 minutes, until the dough is nice and springy.

Place in a lightly oiled bowl and cover with cling film. Leave to prove in the fridge over-night.

The following morning, remove the dough from the fridge and divide into 6 equal pieces. Shape into flattish balls, then place in muffin rings if you have them; otherwise simply space them 2.5cm apart on a tray and leave to prove, covered with cling film or a moistened linen tea towel, for a further hour at room temperature.

Place a non-stick frying pan over a very low heat (you need to cook the muffins through without the outsides burning). Add a knob of butter then cook 2–3 muffins at a time for about 20 minutes on each side.

Serve sliced in half and toasted, with lashings of butter and jam, or with Eggs Benedict and suchlike (see pages 21–31).

Homemade Spelt Crispbreads

We know loads of people claim things are easy to make, but really, these are genuinely easy. You could make a larger quantity of dough and freeze it, defrosting and using it as and when, but as these crispbreads are so quick to put together we prefer to make the perfect amount needed.

Preparation time: 5 minutes
Cooking time: 25 minutes
Makes: 20 crackers

250g spelt flour, plus extra for dusting
½ tsp salt
1 tsp black pepper
150ml tepid water
drizzle of olive oil
1 tbsp seeds, e.g. poppy, sesame, nigella, sunflower, fennel

Preheat the oven to 180°C/gas 4.

Combine the flour, salt and pepper in a bowl. Make a well in the centre and add the water, little by little, mixing it into the flour with your hands. Drizzle over some olive oil, then mix and knead for a minute until you have a shiny, round piece of dough that is not too sticky.

Sprinkle some flour onto a flat baking tray then add the dough. Roll out as thinly as you can, then prick all over with a fork. Score the dough into a grid (this will make it easier to break into neatish crispbreads later on), then sprinkle over some water, followed by the seeds of your choice.

Bake for 25 minutes, or until golden brown. Once cool enough to handle, break into pleasing chunks. These crispbreads will keep happily in an airtight tin for a few days.

Three-ingredient Flatbreads

These slightly tangy flatbreads could not be more simple to put together. They are good to have up your sleeve when you want something to mop up your eggs but a) don't have any bread in and b) can't be bothered to get dressed and buy some.

Preparation time: 5 minutes
Cooking time: Less than 10 minutes
Makes: 4 small or 2 large flatbreads

160g self-raising flour
150g Greek yoghurt
good pinch of salt

Mix together the flour, yoghurt and salt and knead together to form a dough. Divide into four (or two) equal pieces and roll into circles ½cm thick.

Place a frying pan over a medium heat and, when hot, add a couple of dough rounds.

Cook for approximately 3 minutes on each side, until speckled with golden brown spots, then repeat for the second batch. Put on a plate and cover with a tea towel to keep warm before eating.

Home Fries

These little chunks of slightly crisp, red-hued potatoes are more appealing than the ubiquitous greasy spoon chips, not least because they are better at mopping up the yolk of a fried egg. As their name suggests, they are also more suited to cooking at home as there's no irritating deep-frying to sully your kitchen.

If you want to make your home fries into a hash, add some chopped chorizo, crumbled sausage meat or sliced bacon to the pan after you have cooked the peppers. Fry the meat until browned and cooked through, then add to the fried potatoes along with the peppers.

Preparation time: 5 mins
Cooking time: 30–35 minutes
Serves: 4

800g potatoes (we like Rooster red), scrubbed and chopped into 2.5cm cubes
4 tbsp vegetable oil
1 red pepper, chopped a similar size to the potatoes

1 green pepper, chopped a similar size to the potatoes
1 tsp smoked paprika
½–1 tsp cayenne pepper
salt

To serve
4 over-easy fried eggs (see page 12)
hot sauce

Bring a large pan of salted water to the boil. Add the potatoes and simmer until just tender, about 7 minutes. Drain and cool; if making ahead, put in the fridge to chill until ready to use.

Add 1 tablespoon of the oil to a large frying pan over a medium heat. Add the peppers, season with salt and cook, stirring occasionally, for 10–15 minutes, or until softened and a bit charred. Transfer to a bowl.

Add the remaining oil to the pan and when hot, add the potatoes, spices and salt.

Cook over a medium to high heat for around 10–15 minutes. Wait until they form a nice crispy brown crust, then shuffle the pan occasionally or use a wide spatula to turn them (you don't want them to break up). Continue cooking until golden all over and crisp in places.

Return the peppers to the pan for the final couple of minutes and give the pan a little shuffle so that everything melds together. Top each portion with a fried egg and serve with hot sauce.

Their ingredients and cooking methods may vary, but potato pancakes are a traditional food in many countries and cultures. It seems there are few people who don't love a fried potato in some form, and we are no exception.

Latkes are traditionally eaten during the Jewish festival of Hanukkah, but they are delicious any time and work especially well for brunch, pairing perfectly with soft-boiled eggs, smoked or cured fish, a variety of pickles and even – deeply unorthodox as it may be – crispy bacon.

Chutzpah with the seasoning is crucial: an under-seasoned latke will just not taste as good. If you want to err on the side of caution, add a little less seasoning to the mix, fry one pancake to taste, then adjust the uncooked mixture as you like. For jazzier-looking latkes, substitute sweet potato, or replace a couple of the potatoes with beetroot.

Preparation time: 15 minutes
Cooking time: 20–25 minutes
Makes: around 12 large (9cm diameter) latkes, or 24 smaller ones

1kg potatoes, peeled
2 onions
1 tsp baking powder
3 tbsp flour
1 egg

1 tbsp salt
1 tbsp pepper
neutral-flavoured oil, for frying

To serve
soured cream
fish roe
smoked or cured salmon (see page 131)
quick pickled cucumber (see page 183)

Grate the potatoes and onions in a food processor with a grating attachment or by hand with a box grater.

Place a large piece of muslin or a clean tea towel in a colander set over a large bowl. Scrape the potatoes and onions into the cloth, tie together and squeeze out as much liquid as possible. This is key to getting crisp latkes, so squeeze thoroughly.

Tip the potato and onion into a large bowl and mix in the baking powder, flour, egg, salt and pepper until thoroughly combined.

Line a large tray with kitchen paper. Add around ½cm oil to a non-stick pan and place over a medium heat. When hot (drop in a piece of potato to check – if it sizzles quickly, you're ready) add a few heaped tablespoons of latke mix. Squish them down to flatten, then leave for around 3–4 minutes. You don't want to turn them before they've developed a thick enough crust to hold together, so when the little strands of potato at the bottom edge are turning brown they should be good to go. A stainless steel spatula or fish slice is handy for flipping.

(continued overleaf)

Cook the other side for 3–4 minutes, then transfer to the lined tray to drain. Repeat to make a second and third batch.

Ideally, you want to eat the latkes immediately while they are crisp and hot from the pan. But if you want to make them a few hours in advance, place on a wire rack after draining and leave to cool, then cover loosely.

When you're ready to eat, warm through in a preheated oven (160°C/gas 3). Serve with dollops of soured cream topped with fish roe or cured salmon and pickles.

Labneh

We use Greek yoghurt to make labneh, the Middle Eastern strained yoghurt/soft cheese, as we generally have it in the fridge and you can buy it pretty much anywhere. The amount below should be plenty for four people, but you can always increase the quantity – just up the salt to taste. Keep any leftover labneh covered in the fridge, where it should last for 5 days (balls of labneh stored in oil – see below – will keep for longer).

Preparation time: 5 minutes, plus straining
Serves: 4

500g full-fat Greek yoghurt
½–1 tsp fine sea salt (according to taste)

Mix the yoghurt and salt together in a bowl until smooth.

Line a colander with a piece of doubled muslin and place over a large bowl. Spoon the yoghurt into the centre, then bring the edges of the cloth together, twist and tie into a knot. Leave the bundle in the colander, weighing it down with a plate. Alternatively, you can tie the ends of the cheesecloth to something secure, such as a kitchen cupboard handle (make sure it's not a cupboard you want to keep opening), with the bowl positioned underneath.

Leave to strain: 6-ish hours for a soft, spreadable consistency, 12-ish hours for something firmer and similar to cream cheese, or 24+ hours for feta-like crumbliness.

If your labneh is fairly firm, you can roll it little balls and store in a container filled with olive oil and flavoured with chopped herbs, lemon zest and spices.

Homemade Mayonnaise

There will always be a place in our hearts for shop-bought mayo. However, it really is easy to make your own, much easier than, say, a hollandaise, as you don't have the added fear of temperature-related splits. The result is really quite something. Make this for very special bacon sandwiches… on Mother's Day, Father's Day or, if you're feeling compassionate, for someone experiencing the hangover from hell. It will keep in the fridge for a week and would be delicious in homemade coleslaw and with the oeufs mimosa (see pages 120 and 146).

Preparation time: 6 minutes
Makes: 1 large jar (about 350ml)

2 egg yolks
1 tbsp Dijon mustard
100ml rapeseed oil
100ml sunflower oil
50ml extra-virgin olive oil
2 tbsp vinegar
salt and black pepper

Place the egg yolks in a bowl, add the mustard and whisk together. When combined very, very slowly trickle in a tiny bit of rapeseed oil, whisking all the while. Continue until the mixture comes together (our friend Julia swears by whisking in one direction, then the other to speed this process up), then add some more oil. Keep whisking in this way until you have used up all the oils and the mixture is lovely and silky. Add the vinegar and season to taste, then you are good to go.

If your hollandaise splits, don't panic: you can revive it by adding an egg yolk to a bowl with a little splash of water and gradually whisking the mixture into the split sauce.

Preparation time: 5 minutes
Cooking time: 15 minutes
Makes: about 250ml

200g unsalted butter
4 large egg yolks
1 tbsp lemon juice, plus extra to taste
½ tbsp white wine vinegar
fine sea salt, to taste

Take your butter out of the fridge about half an hour before you want to use it and roughly chop into cubes.

Fill a small pan around a third full with water and put over a medium heat until gently simmering, then turn down to low to medium.

Add the egg yolks and the tablespoon of lemon juice to a heatproof bowl and set over the pan, making sure the bottom of the bowl doesn't touch the water. Whisk together – the mixture will quickly start to thicken. Keep whisking, gradually adding the butter bit by bit.

Lower the heat if you're worried the sauce might split, or take the bowl off the pan and whisk off the heat for a moment before returning. Adding the butter too quickly or having the heat too high are the main culprits of split hollandaise.

When all the butter has melted (this shouldn't take more than 8 minutes or so) whisk in the vinegar. Add the extra lemon juice and salt to taste.

This sauce is best served immediately, but you can cover and keep it warm on the lowest of low heats until needed.

10

Hair of the Dog and Thirst Quenchers

Blood Orange Fizz

It's no understatement to say that we look forward to the first bloods of the year (a beacon of joy in the bleak wasteland that is Jan–Feb) with almost hysterical excitement. Adding a little of their bitter-sweet juice to a glass of fizz is a good cure for the winter blues.

Preparation time: 3 minutes
Serves: 1

50ml freshly squeezed blood orange juice
100ml chilled prosecco or other
    sparkling wine

Pour the orange juice into a flute or glass then top up with the prosecco and stir.

Marmalade Martini

We would advise mixing up a breakfast martini only if you have very little to do afterwards, and some soft furnishings nearby on which to sprawl.

Preparation time: 5 minutes
Serves: 1

50ml good-quality gin
15ml lemon juice
1 tbsp marmalade (any type)
ice

Add all the ingredients to a cocktail shaker and shake together, making sure the marmalade has broken up, then add ice and shake again, hard. If the marmalade has dissolved, strain into chilled glasses (if not, shake again).

Banana and Peanut Butter Smoothie

This is a good post-run (or whatever form
of physical torture you put yourself through)
pick-me-up.

Preparation time: 2 minutes
Serves: 1

1 banana
1 tbsp peanut butter
60g natural yoghurt
60ml milk
1 large ice cube

Place all the ingredients in a blender or food
processor and whizz together until fully
combined. Pour into a glass and enjoy.

Peach and Raspberry Smoothie

This fruity smoothie is just the thing in the summer months, when peaches and raspberries are plentiful and you're too hot to feel much like eating (not that this happens to us that frequently).

Preparation time: 5 minutes
Makes: 1 tall glass (about 300ml),
   or 2 smaller glasses

1 ripe peach
100g raspberries
1 tbsp Greek yoghurt
1 large ice cube

Blend all the ingredients together in a food processor or blender until nearly smooth (a few chunks add to the homemade charm), then pour into a glass.

Gazpacho Bloody Mary

Try to get a hold of the smooth, ready-
made gazpacho made Alvalle Gazpacho
(produced by Tropicana) for this delicious
take on the Bloody Mary.

Preparation time: 2 minutes
Serves: 1

2 parts vodka
4 parts gazpacho

dash of Worcestershire sauce
dash of Tabasco
black pepper
squeeze of lemon juice
celery stick, to serve (optional)

Mix all the liquid ingredients together and
serve in a glass over ice with a celery stick,
if liked. Multiply the quantities above to
make a jug of the cocktail.

Watermelon and Cucumber Agua Fresca

Brunch needn't be a booze-fest: this refreshing flavoured water is more quaffable and thirst-quenching than juice, and super simple to make.

Preparation time: 5 minutes
Makes: around 800ml (enough for
    4 glasses)

1 large wedge ripe watermelon
    (600g prepared weight, see below)

1 cucumber (200g prepared weight)
juice of 2 limes
1 tsp agave syrup or honey, to taste
200ml cold water
2 sprigs of mint, leaves picked
ice, to serve

Cut the rind from the melon, roughly chop the flesh and discard any rogue seeds. Peel the skin from the cucumber, then cut the flesh in quarters lengthways. Slice off the majority of the seedy middle and discard. Roughly chop into chunks.

Put the watermelon and cucumber in a blender or food processor and whizz together. Add the lime juice, agave or honey to taste and whizz again. Add the mint leaves and chill for at least 1 hour.

Strain through a sieve to remove most of the mushy pulp (don't worry if a bit gets through) and chill again until needed. Serve with ice.

Orange and Pomegranate Juice

Ubiquitous in Rome cafés, a little sunset-hued glass of this beautiful combination is a real treat for guests deserving of your arm-work (you probably won't be surprised to hear that we do not own juicers). As a rule, one generally needs 3 oranges to make 1 glass of orange juice. Here, with the addition of pomegranate juice, about 2½ per person will do.

The easiest way we've found to juice a pomegranate is to use an Italian manual citrus press like the one pictured opposite. Simply quarter the pomegranate and press, cut sides down, in the contraption to extract the juice, as you would with the orange halves. You'll be surprised at how much juice they yield.

Preparation time: 8 minutes
Serves: 4

1 large pomegranate
10 oranges

Slice the oranges in half and quarter the pomegranate. Begin by pressing the oranges and distribute the juice evenly between four glasses as you go.

Finally, press the pomegranate quarters, and pour on top of the orange juice in the glasses. Pop in the fridge until you are ready to serve.

Mango Lassi

This is the perfect accompaniment to the potato bhaji (see page 49).

Preparation time: 5 minutes
Serves: 1

1 very ripe mango
150ml yoghurt

3 ice cubes
tiny pinch of freshly ground
  cardamom (optional)
squeeze of lime juice, to taste
pinch of caster sugar, to taste

Slice the mango laterally either side of the stone, as close as you can, then make criss-cross incisions in the flesh, without piercing the skin. Push the flesh outwards using your fingers, slice off the chunks and place in a bowl. Salvage any further flesh from around the stone and add to the bowl.

Add the mango to a blender or food processor with the yoghurt, ice cubes and cardamom, if using. Blitz until combined, then add lime juice and sugar to taste. If the mixture needs a little thinning, add a splash of water, then pour into a glass.

Homemade Lemonade

This recipe makes a delicious lemonade, tart and cloudy, and is an attempt at recreating the version we discovered in the now sadly closed Mishkin's restaurant in Covent Garden. Prepare this the night before and serve over lots of ice with slices of cucumber or mint if you wish.

Preparation time: 10 minutes
Serves: 6–8

5 lemons
100g sugar

1.4 litres water
sliced cucumber and mint leaves,
    to serve (optional)
fizzy water, to serve (optional)

Place 2 of the lemons in a blender and pulse until you have a completely smooth paste. Add to a large jug or bowl and follow with the sugar, water and juice from the remaining lemons.

Mix well, allowing the sugar to dissolve, then strain through a sieve or muslin cloth into your serving jug. Mix again before serving over ice, with sliced cucumber or mint leaves, if liked. Add a splash of fizzy water should you wish dilute it further.

Iced Tea

Delightfully retro and so easy to make. Any fruit teabags will do for this, however our favourite is Taylor's rhubarb tea.

Preparation time: 5 minutes, plus chilling
Serves: 6

3 fruit teabags
1 black or breakfast teabag
sugar, to taste

Add the teabags to a large teapot and cover with 1 litre of boiling water. Leave to infuse, removing the black teabag after a few minutes, but leaving the fruit teabags in for a further 5 minutes.

Pour the tea into a jug and add sugar to taste (about 4 or 5 teaspoons is usually enough). Allow to cool, then place in the fridge to chill for 45 minutes. Serve in glasses over ice.

Index

Page references in *italics* indicate photographs.

A

Agua Fresca, Watermelon and Cucumber 204, *205*
All-Day Breakfast Potstickers 65, *66*, 67
American-style Biscuits 61
asparagus:
    Asparagus, Romesco and Egg on Toast 82

Baked Eggs with Asparagus 30
avocados:
    Avocado Toast 76, *77*
    Roasted Citrus and Avocado Salad *134*, 135

B

bacon:
    BLT Buffet Bar *84–5*, 86, *87*
    Devils on Horseback *148*, 149
    Roasted Tomato, Spring Onion and Bacon Quiche 62, *63*, 64
Bagel Brunch *116–17*, 118–19, *119*
Bagels 180, *181*, 182
Baked Arnie Bennie Eggs 29
Baked Beans, Overnight Boston *26*, 27
Baked Bennie 31
Baked Eggs with Asparagus 30
Baked Eggs with Chorizo 97
Baked Eggs with Peppers 96
Baked Eggs with Smoked Salmon 97
bananas:
    Banana and Peanut Butter Smoothie 200
    Coffee and Banana Loaf 161
    Porridge with Rum-caramelised Banana 160
Batter, Pancake or Waffle Buttermilk *34–5*, *36*, 37
Beetroot Pickled Eggs *152*, 153
Bhaji with Cecina, Potato *48*, 49–50

Bircher Muesli *94*, 95
Biscuits, American-style 61
Bistro Salad 132
Blood Orange Fizz 198
Bloody Mary, Gazpacho *202*, 203
BLT Buffet Bar *84–5*, 86, *87*
Blueberry and Rhubarb Muffins *162*, 163
bottomless brunch 100–25
Breakfast Burritos 53
Brioche French Toast 32, *33*
Brisket Buns 120, *121*
brunch 6, 10
    brunches of the world 11
    condiments and *8–9*, 11
    cook's notes 11
    history of 10
Bruschette, Fresh 74, *75*
Bun Cha, Sausage *138*, 139
buns:
    Brisket Buns 120, *121*
    Cinnamon Buns with Cream Cheese Icing *170–1*, 172, 173
Burritos, Breakfast 53

C

Caesar Salad 133
Carrot and Courgette Salad *178*, 179
cheese:
    Cheese and Spring Onion Toastie 83
    Cheese, Ham and Egg Buckwheat
    Galettes 28
    Chilli Cheese Toast 80, *81*
    Cinnamon Buns with Cream Cheese
      Icing *170–1*, 172, 173
    Mediterranean Salad with Quick
      Caponata and Goats' Cheese Toasts
      58, 59, 60
    Sweet Potato and Feta Salad *51*
    Welsh Rabbit 147
Cherry Compote, Sour *166*, 167
Chicken and Honey Mustard Lettuce Wraps,
    Fried *102*, 103–4
Chickpeas with Greens 136, *137*

Chilli Cheese Toast 80, *81*
Chip Butty, Classy 43
Cinnamon Buns with Cream Cheese Icing
    170–1, 172, 173
Citrus and Avocado Salad, Roasted
    134, 135
classics, the 18–45
Classy Chip Butty 43
Coffee and Banana Loaf 161
compote:
    Sour Cherry Compote *166*, 167
    Spiced Rhubarb Compote 168, *169*
condiments *8–9*, 11
Continental, The *122–3*
cook's notes 11
Crispbreads, Homemade Spelt 186
Cured Salmon, Three Ways 131

D

Devilled Eggs *144*, 145
Devils on Horseback *148*, 149

E

eggs 12, 13
    Asparagus, Romesco and Egg on Toast
      82
    Baked Arnie Bennie Eggs 29
    Baked Bennie 31
    Baked Eggs with Asparagus 30
    Baked Eggs with Chorizo 97

    Baked Eggs with Peppers 96
    Baked Eggs with Smoked Salmon 97
    Beetroot Pickled Eggs *152*, 153
    boiled 13, 16
    Cheese, Ham and Egg Buckwheat
      Galettes 28
    coddled 16

Devilled Eggs *144*, 145
Eggs Benedict *20*, 21
fried 13, *14–15*, *17*
Green Scrambled Eggs 92
Leek and Taleggio Tartine 73
Masala Omelette *24*, 25
Menemen 93
Mexican Scrambled Egg Tacos 52
More Baked Eggs, Three Ways 96, 97
'Nduja and Egg Pizza *110–11*, 112–13
Oeufs Mimosa 146
poached 16

Poached Eggs with Yoghurt and Chilli
   Butter *90*, 91
Quesadilla'd Huevos Rancheros *54*,
   55, 56
Sausage and Egg Muffin *78*, 79
Scotch Woodcock 151
scrambled 13
Shakshuka 22, *23*
Veggie Scotch Eggs 154, *155*
English Muffins *184*, 185
extras 174–95

F

Falafel with Baba Ghanoush, Lentil 114–15
Flatbreads, Three-ingredient 187
French Toast, Brioche 32, *33*
fresh and light(er) 126–41
Fresh Bruschette 74, *75*
Fried Chicken and Honey Mustard Lettuce
   Wraps *102*, 103–4

Fries, Home *188*, 189
Frittata, Spaghetti 98, *99*
Fruit Salads 140, *141*
Fry-Up, A Veggie with Homemade
   Hash Brown *40*, 41–2
Ful Egyptian, The *128*, 129–30
Full English, The No Frills 44, *45*

G

Galettes, Cheese, Ham and Egg
   Buckwheat 28
Gazpacho Bloody Mary *202*, 203
Granola *158*, 159
Green Scrambled Eggs 92

H

hair of the dog & thirst quenchers 196–211
Hollandaise 195
Home Fries *188*, 189
Homemade Lemonade 209

Homemade Mayonnaise 194
Homemade Spelt Crispbreads 186
Huevos Rancheros, Quesadilla'd *54*, 55, 56

I

Iced Tea 210

J

Jacket Potato Spread 105, *106–7*, 108, *109*
Jerusalem Salad 176, *177*

K

Kippers with Bread and Butter, Smoked 150

L

Labneh 193
Latkes *190*, 191–26
Leek and Taleggio Tartine 73

Lemonade, Homemade 209
Lentil Falafel with Baba Ghanoush 114–15
Loaf, Coffee and Banana 161

M

Mackerel Pâté with Pickles 183
Mango Lassi 208
Marmalade Martini 199
Martini, Marmalade 199
Masala Omelette *24*, 25
Mayonnaise, Homemade 194
Mediterranean Salad with Quick Caponata
    and Goats' Cheese Toasts 58, *59*, 60
Menemen 93

Mexican Scrambled Egg Tacos 52
modern medleys 46–67
More Baked Eggs, Three Ways 96, 97
Muesli, Bircher *94*, 95
muffins:
    Blueberry and Rhubarb Muffins *162*, 163
    English Muffins *184*, 185
    Sausage and Egg Muffin *78*, 79

N

'Nduja and Egg Pizza *110–11*, 112–13
No Frills Full English, The 44, *45*

O

Oeufs Mimosa 146
Omelette, Masala *24*, 25
oranges:
    Blood Orange Fizz 198
    Orange and Pomegranate Juice *206*, 207
Overnight Boston Baked Beans *26*, 27

P

Pancake or Waffle Buttermilk Batter 34–5,
36, 37
Pâté with Pickles, Mackerel 183
Peach and Raspberry Smoothie 201
Pizza, 'Nduja and Egg *110–11*, 112–13
Poached Eggs with Yoghurt and Chilli Butter
90, 91
porridge:
Porridge with Rum-caramelised
Banana 160
Scottish-style Porridge 38, *39*

potatoes:
Jacket Potato Spread 105, *106–7*,
108, *109*
Latkes *190*, 191–26
Potato Bhaji with Cecina *48*, 49–50
Spiced Potato Cakes with Watercress
and Quail Egg Salad 57
Sweet Potato and Feta Salad 51
Veggie Fry-Up with Homemade Hash
Brown, A *40*, 41–2
Potstickers, All-Day Breakfast 65, *66*, 67

Q

Quesadilla'd Huevos Rancheros *54*, 55, 56
Quiche, Roasted Tomato, Spring Onion
and Bacon 62, *63*, 64
quick ideas for one or two 88–99

R

rhubarb:
Blueberry and Rhubarb Muffins *162*, 163
Spiced Rhubarb Compote 168, *169*
Roasted Citrus and Avocado Salad *134*, 135
Roasted Tomato, Spring Onion and
Bacon Quiche 62, *63*, 64

S

Sabich *70*, 71, 72
salads:
    Bistro Salad 132
    Caesar Salad 133
    Carrot and Courgette Salad *178*, 179
    Jerusalem Salad 176, *177*
    Mediterranean Salad with Quick
        Caponata and Goats' Cheese Toasts
        58, 59, 60
    Roasted Citrus and Avocado Salad
        134, 135
    Spiced Potato Cakes with Watercress
        and Quail Egg Salad 57
    Sweet Potato and Feta Salad 51
Salmon, Cured Three Ways 131
sandwiches, tartines, toasties & 68–87
sausage:
    Sausage and Egg Muffin *78*, 79
    Sausage Bun Cha *138*, 139

savouries 142–55
Scandinental, The *124–5*
Scotch Eggs, Veggie 154, *155*
Scotch Woodcock 151
Scottish-style Porridge 38, *39*
Shakshuka 22, *23*
Smoked Kippers with Bread and Butter 150
smoothies:
    Banana and Peanut Butter Smoothie 200
    Peach and Raspberry Smoothie 201
Sour Cherry Compote *166*, 167
Spaghetti Frittata 98, *99*
Spelt Crispbreads, Homemade 186
Spiced Potato Cakes with Watercress
    and Quail Egg Salad 57
Spiced Rhubarb Compote 168, *169*
Sweet Potato and Feta Salad 51
sweet spot, that 156–73

T

Tacos, Mexican Scrambled Egg 52
Tartine, Leek and Taleggio 73
tartines, toasties & sandwiches 68–87
Tea, Iced 210
Three-ingredient Flatbreads 187
toast:
    Asparagus, Romesco and Egg
        on Toast 82
    Avocado Toast 76, *77*
    Brioche French Toast 32, *33*

    Cheese and Spring Onion Toastie 83
    Chilli Cheese Toast 80, *81*
    Mediterranean Salad with Quick
        Caponata and Goats' Cheese
        Toasts 58, *59*, 60
tomatoes:
    BLT Buffet Bar *84–5*, 86, *87*
    Roasted Tomato, Spring Onion
        and Bacon Quiche 62, *63*, 64

V

Veggie Fry-Up with Homemade Hash Brown,
  A *40*, 41–2
Veggie Scotch Eggs 154, *155*

W

Waffle Buttermilk Batter *34–5*, *36*, 37
Watermelon and Cucumber Agua Fresca
  204, *205*
Welsh Rabbit 147
world, brunches of the 11
Wraps, Fried Chicken and Honey Mustard
  Lettuce *102*, 103–4

Acknowledgements

Thank you to:

Our publishers, Square Peg – the wonderful Rowan Yapp, Rosemary Davidson and Susannah Otter – for coming up with this idea and being so enthusiastic about it. Also to Louise Court, Nick Skidmore, Clare Sayer and Trish Burgess for all your hard work.

Special mention to our excellent editor Rowan, owner of the most elegant hands in publishing, for lending her fair appendages and hollandaise-making skills at the photoshoots – and to Susannah for learning to pleat like a dumpling pro and being generally fabulous.

Our agent, Jon Elek, and also Millie Hoskins, at United Agents for their support, all the nitty gritty things they do for us, and for always being enthusiastic, constructive tasters.

Liz and Max Haarala Hamilton for the brilliant photos, being so much fun to work with, and letting us cover their kitchen counters with eggs.

James Ward for the fantastic design.

Becca, Daisy and Max aka The Dusty Knuckle Bakery for sharing their dough wisdom. Françoise Craig, for her diligent recipe testing. Paul Missing for chickpea recipe testing once again, and Debbie and Jake Missing for general support. And to all those we've shared happy brunches with: you know who you are.

Self-indulgent as it may sound, thanks to each other. It's more than five years since we first bumped office chairs while working back to back at the same publishing house, and we feel very lucky that cooking and eating first brought us together and continues to do so.

About the Authors

Caroline Craig has written for the *Guardian* and is the co-author of *The Little Book of Lunch, The Cornershop Cookbook,* and *The Kew Gardens Children's Cookbook*. Her maternal family have been fruit farmers and wine producers in Provence for generations. A childhood spent gobbling home-grown tomatoes and peaches left her with little choice but to shape her life around delicious food and cooking for friends and family.

Sophie Missing is a writer and editor who started her career in publishing at Hodder & Stoughton and Penguin. She has written for the *Guardian*, the *Observer*, and *MUNCHIES*, and is the co-author of two previous cookbooks, *The Little Book of Lunch* and *The Cornershop Cookbook*. She lives in London.

1 3 5 7 9 10 8 6 4 2

Square Peg, an imprint of Vintage,
 20 Vauxhall Bridge Road,
London SW1V 2SA

Square Peg is part of the Penguin Random House group of companies
whose addresses can be found at global.penguinrandomhouse.com

Penguin
Random House
UK

First published by Square Peg in 2017

Penguin.co.uk/vintage

A CIP catalogue record for this book is available from the British Library

ISBN 9781910931448

Design by James Ward
Photography by Haarala Hamilton
Food and Prop Styling by Sophie Missing and Caroline Craig

Printed and bound by Toppan Leefung Printing Ltd

Penguin Random House is committed to a sustainable future for
our business, our readers and our planet. This book is made from
Forest Stewardship Council® certified paper.

MIX
Paper from
responsible sources
FSC® C018179